Cambridge Elements ≡

Elements in Politics and Society in Latin America
edited by
Maria Victoria Murillo
Columbia University
Juan Pablo Luna
The Pontifical Catholic University of Chile
Tulia G. Falleti
University of Pennsylvania
Andrew Schrank
Brown University

UNDERSTANDING INSTITUTIONAL WEAKNESS

Power and Design in Latin American Institutions

Daniel M. Brinks
University of Texas at Austin

Steven Levitsky
Harvard University

Maria Victoria Murillo
Columbia University

CAMBRIDGE
UNIVERSITY PRESS

CAMBRIDGE
UNIVERSITY PRESS

University Printing House, Cambridge CB2 8BS, United Kingdom

One Liberty Plaza, 20th Floor, New York, NY 10006, USA

477 Williamstown Road, Port Melbourne, VIC 3207, Australia

314–321, 3rd Floor, Plot 3, Splendor Forum, Jasola District Centre,
New Delhi – 110025, India

79 Anson Road, #06–04/06, Singapore 079906

Cambridge University Press is part of the University of Cambridge.

It furthers the University's mission by disseminating knowledge in the pursuit of
education, learning, and research at the highest international levels of excellence.

www.cambridge.org
Information on this title: www.cambridge.org/9781108738880
DOI: 10.1017/9781108772211

First published 2019

A catalogue record for this publication is available from the British Library.

ISBN 978-1-108-73888-0 Paperback
ISSN 2515-5245 (print)
ISSN 2515-5253 (online)

Understanding Institutional Weakness

Power and Design in Latin American Institutions

Elements in Politics and Society in Latin America

DOI: 10.1017/9781108772211
First published online: August 2019

Daniel M. Brinks
University of Texas at Austin

Steven Levitsky
Harvard University

Maria Victoria Murillo
Columbia University

Author for correspondence: Maria Victoria Murillo mm2140@columbia.edu

Abstract: This Element introduces the concept of institutional weakness, arguing that weakness or strength is a function of the extent to which an institution actually matters to social, economic, or political outcomes. It then presents a typology of three forms of institutional weakness: insignificance, in which rules are complied with but do not affect the way actors behave; noncompliance, in which state elites either choose not to enforce the rules or fail to gain societal cooperation with them; and instability, in which the rules are changed at an unusually high rate. The Element then examines the sources of institutional weakness.

Keywords: institutions, Latin America, enforcement, compliance, instability

ISBNs: 9781108738880 (PB), 9781108772211 (OC)
ISSNs: 2515-5245 (print), 2515-5253 (online)

Contents

1 Introduction*

Latin America has long been a source of frustration for students of political institutions. The region has a lengthy constitutional history. Most Latin American states adopted republican constitutions nearly two centuries ago. Yet these new institutions were superimposed on societies marked by weak states and vast socioeconomic, ethnic, and regional inequalities. The result was often a dramatic gap between the rules that were written on parchment and the way politics worked in practice, as postcolonial elites engaged in discrimination, manipulation, and evasion in applying laws. The tension between the promise of political equality and the realities of economic and social inequality was a constant source of regime instability. Constitutions were repeatedly scrapped and rewritten (Elkins et al. 2009), suspended for months or even years via "states of exception" (Loveman 1994), or flatly ignored. In many countries, this inaugurated a pattern of institutional weakness that endured into the twentieth century. The failure of parchment rules to generate desired or expected outcomes frustrated scholars and policymakers alike. Indeed, by the time Latin America succumbed to a wave of authoritarianism in the 1960s and 1970s, many scholars of the region had concluded that political institutions mattered little.

The Third Wave of democratization brought the study of institutions back to the fore. By the late 1990s, every country in Latin America except Cuba was at least nominally a presidential democracy with a range of new constitutional rights empowering its citizens. Once again, scholars and policymakers sought to design (or borrow) institutions that would enhance the stability and quality of democracy amid pervasive social inequalities. Yet these newly minted parchment rules often failed to generate the outcomes their designers expected or hoped for. Constitutional checks and balances did not always constrain presidents (O'Donnell 1994). Nominally independent judiciaries and central banks often lacked teeth in practice,[1] and electoral reforms had little effect on party systems (Remmer 2008). Newly enshrined social rights were often not

* Many of the ideas and illustrations in this Element are drawn from the edited volume *The Politics of Institutional Weakness in Latin America* (Brinks, Levitsky, and Murillo, forthcoming). We are grateful for the suggestions of all the participants in the conferences at Harvard (2015) and the University of Texas at Austin (2017) as well as Kathleen Thelen, Peter Hall, Ira Katznelson, participants at seminars in Universidad de San Andres and Universidad de San Martin, and two anonymous reviewers. We are also thankful for the financial support of the David Rockefeller Center for Latin American Studies and the Weatherhead Center for International Affairs at Harvard University, the Bernard and Audre Rapoport Center for Human Rights and Justice at the University of Texas, Austin, and the Institute for Latin American Studies at Columbia University.
[1] Cukierman et al. (1992); Bill Chavez (2004); Helmke (2004); Brinks and Blass (2017).

respected in practice (Gauri and Brinks 2008). Presidential term limits were circumvented or overturned.[2] Civil service laws (Grindle 2012; Gingerich 2013), tax laws (Bergman 2009), labor and environmental regulations,[3] and laws prohibiting squatting and street vending (Holland and Hummell 2017) were enforced unevenly, if at all. Whether it was due to extreme instability, uneven enforcement, or both, the relationship between formal rules and expected outcomes remained weak in many Third Wave Latin American democracies. Yet there also existed considerable variation – across countries, across institutions within countries, and over time – in both the durability of parchment institutions and their capacity to shape actors' behavior.

This variation is consequential. Institutional weakness narrows actors' time horizons in ways that can undermine both economic performance (Spiller and Tommasi 2007) and the stability and quality of democracy (O'Donnell 1994). Democracy requires that laws be applied evenly, across territory and across diverse categories of citizens. That is, every citizen should be equal before the law, notwithstanding inequalities created by markets and societies. Institutional weakness undermines that equality – and it hinders efforts to use laws and public policies to combat the multifaceted inequalities that continue to plague much of Latin America. Institutions are not uniformly positive; laws create inequalities as often as they combat them. They may be exclusionary or discriminatory, reinforce inequality or other societal injustices, or – as Albertus and Menaldo (2018) show – protect authoritarian elites and their interests. In some cases, full democratization may require weakening and replacing such institutions. In general, however, no democracy can function well without strong institutions.

Although the problem of institutional weakness is now widely recognized in the field of comparative politics, it has not been adequately conceptualized or theorized. We do not yet have a clear conceptual framework that allows us to identify, measure, and compare different forms of institutional weakness. Such a framework is essential if we are to build theories about the sources and consequences of institutional weakness. In this Element, we take an initial step toward such a framework by presenting a typology of distinct forms of institutional weakness and exploring the potential sources of that weakness.

1.1 Why Institutional Strength Matters for Comparative Politics

Recent research on Latin American politics makes manifest the need to broaden the comparative scope of institutional analysis and theorize institutional

---

[2] Helmke (2017); Pérez-Liñán (2007); Corrales and Penfold (2014).

[3] See Bensusán (2000); Piore and Schrank (2008); Ronconi (2010); Murillo, Ronconi, and Schrank (2011); Coslovsky (2011); and Amengual (2014).

weakness. Take, for example, Gretchen Helmke's (2004) study of executive–judicial relations in Argentina. Established theories of judicial politics – which draw heavily on the case of the United States – tell us that lifetime tenure security for Supreme Court justices should enable justices to act with political independence. But when rules of tenure security are routinely violated in such a way that justices know that voting against the executive could trigger their removal, judicial behavior changes markedly. Helmke finds that when institutions of tenure security are weak, as in Argentina during much of the twentieth century, justices are more likely to vote with presidents during the early part of their term. As the president's term in office concludes, however, justices tend to engage in "strategic defection," ruling in line with the party or politician they expect to succeed the outgoing president (Helmke 2004). Thus, Helmke identifies – and theorizes – a pattern of judicial behavior that is based on the expectation of institutional weakness and diverges markedly from what would be expected in a strong institutional context.

Alisha Holland's (2017) work on forbearance and redistribution similarly highlights the importance of taking variation in enforcement seriously. Most analyses of redistributive politics in Latin America focus on formal social policies such as public pension and health care spending. By such measures, redistributive efforts in the region are strikingly low: social expenditure as a percentage of gross domestic product (GDP) is barely half the Organisation for Economic Co-operation and Development (OECD) average, and unlike most OECD countries, taxes and transfers only marginally reduce income inequality (Holland 2017: 69–70). In unequal democracies such as those in much of Latin America, the persistence of such small welfare states may seem puzzling. By adding the dimension of forbearance, or deliberate non-enforcement of the law, Holland provides a powerful insight into why such outcomes persist. The state's toleration of illegal activities such as squatting and street vending distributes considerable resources to the poor (Holland estimates that in Lima, it amounts to around $750 million a year [2017: 9]). Thus, whereas most Latin American states do little, in formal terms, to support housing and employment for the poor, nonenforcement of laws against squatting and street vending creates an "informal welfare state," in which "downward redistribution happens by the state's leave, rather than through the state's hand" (Holland 2017: 11).

Forbearance toward the poor has thus powerfully shaped long-run welfare state development in Latin America. Because forbearance entails less taxation than formal redistribution, the nonpoor (and governments) may come to prefer it; and when the poor organize around preserving forbearance, popular demands for formal redistribution are often dampened. This "forbearance trap" can lock in informal welfare states for decades (Holland 2017: 237–276). A central lesson from Holland's work, then, is that understanding the politics of redistribution in unequal democracies requires a focus not only on policy design but also on enforcement.[4]

Alison Post's (2014) research on foreign and domestic investment in infrastructure in Argentina offers another example of how variation in institutional strength shapes policy outcomes. Foreign multinationals – with their deep pockets and long time horizons – are widely expected to hold an advantage over domestic corporations in winning and sustaining favorable infrastructure contracts where institutional veto points constrain governments from modifying the rules (Levy and Spiller 1996; Henisz 2002; Cox and McCubbins 2002) or international third-party enforcement is included in contracts (Elkins et al. 2006; Buthe and Milner 2008). However, Post shows that in weak institutional environments, this is often not the case. In a context of high economic and political volatility, where governments are able to alter the terms of contracts regardless of formal rules, domestic investors with extensive linkages to local economies and politicians are better positioned to sustain and, when necessary, renegotiate contacts.[5] Such "informal contractual supports" may be of little consequence in an institutional environment with strong property rights. However, in a context of institutional instability, such as Argentina in the 2000s, they help explain why domestic investments often prevail over foreign ones (Post 2014). Post thus shows how the behavior of both governments and investors changes in a weak institutional environment, producing investment outcomes that differ markedly from those predicted by the existing literature.

Attention to institutional instability has also reshaped our understanding of electoral design. Most comparative scholarship in this area assumes that those who design the electoral rules do so with a self-interested goal: to maximize their electoral advantage. The most influential work in this area assumed that politicians engage in *far-sighted* institutional design. In other words, they design electoral rules in pursuit of relatively long-term goals (Rokkan 1970; Rogowski 1987; Boix 1999). Boix (1999), for example, argues that conservative elites in much of early twentieth-century Europe replaced plurality electoral systems with proportional representation (PR) systems in an effort to minimize

---

[4] Variation in enforcement should also influence individual preferences over social policy, in line with Mares' (2005) finding that prior individual experience with state institutions affects policy preferences. The social policy literature would benefit from adding variation in enforcement to the range of strategies available to politicians, just as it benefited from focusing on the effects of hidden change despite formal institutional continuity (Hacker 2005; Palier 2005).

[5] Such renegotiation often entails cross-sectoral bargains that violate rules governing market concentration and conflict of interest (Post 2014; Post and Murillo 2016).

their losses in the face of the growing electoral strength of socialist parties. Such theories of far-sighted design hinge on some critical assumptions: for example, actors must believe that the rules they design will endure over the medium to long run; and they must have some certainty that they themselves will remain viable and thus be able to play by those rules. In other words, far-sighted designers of electoral rules must be able to "predict with some certainty the future structure of electoral competition" (Boix 1999: 622). Neither of these assumptions holds in weak institutional environments. Where electoral volatility is high, and where institutions are easily and frequently replaced, far-sighted institutional design is more difficult. In such a context, rule designers remain self-interested, but they are less likely to be far-sighted. Rather, as scholars such as Karen Remmer (2008) and Calvo and Negretto (forthcoming) argue, politicians are more likely to design rules aimed at locking in short-term electoral advantages. Such short-sighted design may well have the effect of reinforcing institutional instability. Allowing for variation in rule designers' time horizons should, therefore, enhance the external validity of theories of institutional design, facilitating their application across different national contexts.

Finally, attention to variation in institutional strength has yielded new insights into the dynamics of institutional change. Recent work in the historical institutionalist tradition has focused attention on forms of gradual institutional change emerging from the reinterpretation or slow redeployment of existing written rules (Streeck and Thelen 2005; Mahoney and Thelen 2010). This scholarship was a useful response to an earlier literature that emphasized discontinuous change – moments of dramatic and far-reaching change, followed by long periods of path-dependent stasis (Krasner 1988). Yet the patterns of layering, drift, conversion, and exhaustion identified by Kathleen Thelen and her collaborators operate in a context of strong formal institutions. As we have argued elsewhere (Levitsky and Murillo 2009, 2014), the dynamics of institutional change can be quite different in a weak institutional environment. Rather than being characterized by "stickiness,"[6] institutional change tends to be rapid and thoroughgoing, often following a pattern of serial replacement, in which rules and procedures are replaced wholesale – without ever settling into a stable equilibrium (Levitsky and Murillo 2014).

Second, actors in a weak institutional environment may achieve real substantive change by modifying enforcement or compliance levels rather than changing the rules. Mahoney and Thelen (2010) have shown how gaps in compliance can serve as a mechanism of hidden change via the subtle

---

[6] For example, Streeck and Thelen (2005) explicitly assume the "stickiness of institutional structures" (p. 18) in their discussion of economic liberalization in advanced democracies.

reinterpretation of institutional goals, even as formal institutional structures remain intact. Building on this insight, recent scholarship shows how the "activation" of previously dormant institutions can be an important source of change (see Levitsky and Murillo 2014). For instance, Saffon and González Bertomeu's (forthcoming) analysis of property rights in Porfirian Mexico shows how changing patterns of enforcement may have far-reaching consequences without altering the letter of the law.[7] At the same time, noncompliance may also be a source of formal institutional *stability*, especially when it tempers an institution's distributive consequences (Levitsky and Murillo 2014).[8] During the 1990s, for example, Latin American governments seeking more flexible labor markets weakened enforcement of existing labor laws while keeping them on the books (Bensusán 2000; Cook 2010).

Recent research thus suggests the need for a more conscious focus on institutional weakness as an object of study rather than as a sort of "random error" that obstructs proper institutional analysis. That is what this Element seeks to do.

1.2 Why Latin America?

Institutional weakness is widespread in the developing and postcommunist worlds. Why, then, examine a single region? We focus on Latin America because it contains both an important set of shared characteristics and useful variation. With few exceptions, Latin American countries possess at least minimally effective states and competitive electoral (if not always fully democratic) regimes. Thus, these are not cases in which political institutions can be dismissed as predictably and uniformly meaningless. Moreover, the region contains within it substantial variation on the dimension of institutional strength – across countries, across institutions, and over time. A focus on Latin America allows us to exploit this variation, while simultaneously benefiting from the scholarship of a relatively close-knit community of scholars with a shared knowledge of the region's history and individual cases. At the same time, the implications drawn from the study of Latin America have clear applicability to other regions of the world, and we expect our framework and the lessons to contribute to a broader debate on political institutions in comparative politics.

---

[7] Latin America exhibits more far-reaching instances of deactivation and activation than what is suggested by Mahoney and Thelen (2010), as political actors are not necessarily restricted to the discretion given by the letter of the law. Processes of activation and deactivation may also be reversed. Holland (2017, forthcoming) shows how electoral incentives drive the shifting activation and deactivation of street vending regulations in Bogota, Lima, and Santiago de Chile.

[8] For example, during a 2018 debate on reforming the rules banning abortion in Argentina, supporters of the existing abortion ban argued that reform was not necessary because no women were actually penalized for terminating their pregnancies (www.lanacion.com.ar /2157341-aborto-no-faltar-a-la-verdad).

Issues of institutional strength are of great consequence in Latin America. Given the region's vast inequalities and state deficiencies, the potential impact of institutional reform *on paper* is often strikingly high. If laws aimed at eliminating corruption, clientelism, racial discrimination, or violence against women, or rules designed to redistribute income to the poor, enforce property rights against squatters, or protect the environment, were *actually complied with over time*, the social and distributional consequences would be enormous. So the stakes of institutional compliance and durability are high. Struggles over whether and how the rules are enforced, and whether they remain on the books or are discarded, have prominent winners and losers. Scholars must better understand what drives these struggles – and what determines their outcomes.

Although this Element focuses on Latin America, its lessons travel beyond the region. The creation of institutions that seem designed to produce low compliance or which fail to generate a coalition that can sustain compliance are hardly unique to Latin America. Incentives to create weak institutions and shared expectations of institutional weakness are endemic across the Global South. Indeed, they may be found in industrialized democracies as well. Thus, the power struggles underlying the design, implementation, and persistence of weak institutions is relevant not only for Latin America but for comparative politics more broadly.

2 Defining Institutions

Before we conceptualize weak institutions, we must define institutions. Most institutionalists begin with North's (1990: 3, 4) definition of institutions as "the humanly devised constraints that shape human interaction ... [in ways that are] perfectly analogous to the rules of the game in a competitive team sport" (see, e.g., Peters 1999: 146). In previous work (Brinks 2003; Helmke and Levitsky 2006), some of us have argued that institutions are made up of rules, and, in the context of defining informal institutions, we have sought to differentiate rules from purely descriptive statements or expectations about behavior. For this project, we adopt the same starting point – the notion that (formal) institutions are made up of (formal) rules. This allows us to focus on formal constraints that are "humanly devised" and recognized as compulsory within a polity. As we will see, these formal constraints interact in complex ways with social norms and other informal institutions, which affects both the work that institutions do and their potential strength or weakness. At the definitional stage, however, we can limit our purview to formal rules.

Many definitions stop there, but for our purposes we must push the definition beyond the implicit equation of institutions with single stand-alone rules or laws. In all cases, we are concerned with the effectiveness of sets of rules rather than with that of single rules in isolation, and with the actors whose conduct is affected by these rules, even though a single rule may sometimes stand in as shorthand for the institution as a whole.

We therefore define a formal institution as a set of officially sanctioned rules that structures human behavior and expectations around a particular activity or goal. Elinor Ostrom (1986: 5) initially defined institutions as "the result of implicit or explicit efforts by a set of individuals to achieve order and predictability within defined situations by: (1) creating positions; (2) stating how participants enter or leave positions; (3) stating which actions participants in these positions are required, permitted, or forbidden to take; and (4) stating which outcome participants are required, permitted, or forbidden to affect." She later added rules that specify (5) the consequences of rule violation, which in most cases we expect to be associated to a specific sanction (Crawford and Ostrom 1995).[9] We simplify Crawford and Ostrom's "grammar" somewhat, defining a formal institution as a set of formal rules structuring human behavior and expectations around a statutory goal by (1) specifying actors and their roles; (2) requiring, permitting, or prohibiting certain behaviors; and (3) defining the consequences of complying or not complying with the remaining rules.

Our conceptual scheme relies on identifying the statutory goal of formal institutions – the second element in our definition above. As we will see in the next section, a strong institution is one that sets a nontrivial goal and achieves it, while a weak institution achieves little or nothing either because it fails to achieve an ambitious goal or because it never set out to accomplish anything. We set statutory goals rather than the (stated or implicit) policy objectives of institutional creators as the benchmark because we recognize that the ultimate policy aim of institutions – often a product of compromise among distinct and even competing interests – may well be ambiguous or contested (Moe 1990; Schickler 2001; Streeck and Thelen 2005; Mahoney and Thelen 2010). By taking the statutory goal itself as a starting point, we can more easily identify how the preferences and strategies of actors work to weaken or strengthen institutions. Whether the institution succeeds in achieving its policy objective or produces extensive unintended consequences can be analyzed separately under more conventional policy effectiveness rubrics. It is entirely possible,

---

[9] Other definitions identify rules specifying roles, thus constituting decision makers; rules that permit, prohibit, or require certain behavior; and rules that define consequences (Hart 1961; Ellickson 1991).

in this conceptual scheme, that a strong institution nevertheless fails to achieve the policy objectives that prompted its creation or does more harm than good in the overall scheme of things.

For instance, Amengual and Dargent (forthcoming) examine the regulatory framework around mining, construction, and agroindustry in Argentina, Bolivia, and Peru. The mining regulations they study have the policy goal of reducing environmental hazards for the local population and the express statutory goal of requiring or forbidding certain practices. The motivation for the mining companies that help enforce these rules might be to access international markets or inhibit competition from informal miners who do not have the technology to fulfill those standards, rather than to protect the environment. Indeed, these motivations are often crucial for understanding firms' incentives to coproduce enforcement. But to measure the strength of the institution, we should examine whether the required or forbidden practices are taking place, not whether the policy goals are being achieved, or whether the mining companies are realizing their objectives. When evaluating institutional strength, then, the focus should be on the ostensible goal of the institution, not on the (public or private) motives of the politicians and other social actors behind it.

Institutional goals may be *transformative*, in that they seek to move outcomes away from the status quo, or *conservative*, in that they seek to preserve the status quo in the face of potential change. This Element focuses primarily on transformative institutions, both because they are more often the subject of political and policy debates in Latin America and because they are more often identified as being weak. Nevertheless, conservative or status quo–preserving institutions can be of great importance. Property laws and civil or criminal codes that enshrine traditional gender roles and family structures are examples. Albertus and Menaldo's (2018) work on the persistence of authoritarian constitutions that protect wealthy elites from redistribution by constraining democratic governments demonstrates that conservative institutions are endemic. The conceptual scheme we propose works in either case. Whether conservative or transformative, institutions are meant to make it more likely that social, economic, or political outcomes will be closer to a defined statutory goal than to some less preferred alternative outcome.

Weak formal institutions should not be confused with informal rules, or those that are "created and enforced outside officially sanctioned channels" (Helmke and Levitsky 2006: 5). Informal institutions may coexist with either strong or weak formal institutions. When they coexist with weak formal institutions, they may either reinforce them by providing a second mechanism that promotes the expected behavior ("substitutive") or undermine them by promoting an alternative behavior ("competing") (Helmke and Levitsky 2006: 14).

Although we recognize (and discuss below) the importance of informal rules in generating institutional strength or weakness, our focus here is on formal institutions.

Finally, it is important to distinguish formal institutions, or rules, from the organizations that are either the targets of those rules (political parties, interest groups, economic actors) or dedicated to enforcing or implementing the rules (bureaucracies). By keeping rules and organizations conceptually distinct, we can evaluate whether strengthening state agencies – hiring more inspectors, spending more on training bureaucratic personnel, buying more vehicles, or establishing meritocratic criteria – actually enhances compliance with the institution, as do Ronconi (2010), Amengual (2016), and Schrank (2011) in their work on labor regulations and civil service.

3 Institutional Weakness

3.1 The Core Concept

After defining formal institutions, we turn to conceptualizing their weakness. We expect strong institutions to redistribute and refract power, authority, or expectations in order to produce an institutional outcome (*io*, in Figure 1) that diverges from what the preinstitutional outcome (*po*) would have been.[10] An institution may be designed to produce an outcome (shown in Figure 1 as *io'*) that is more ambitious than that which it actually produces. A strong institution, however, makes a difference because the distance between *io* and *po* – a parameter we call S (for strength) – is greater than zero. S is a cost to those who prefer *po* and is exactly the benefit sought by those who prefer *io* or *io.'*

We can use the following graph to illustrate this point and set up a vocabulary to use as shorthand:

It is important to note that the move from *po* to *io* is not a move from the state of nature to an institutionalized context. Indeed, *po* could be (in the case of a conservative institution) a feared future outcome the institution is designed to prevent, and *io* may be the status quo it seeks to preserve. The idea is that the

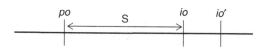

Figure 1: Strong institution – io-$po \gg 0$

---

[10] We use "preinstitutional" here in the same sense in which people commonly use "prepolitical." It is not meant to imply temporality, but rather simply what might happen in the absence of the institution.

institution of interest has been added to the array of interlocking institutions that impinge on any given social and political activity in hopes of producing a particular outcome that might not otherwise obtain, either currently or in the future. The comparison point is a counterfactual – our best estimate of what might happen if the institution were to disappear or be replaced.

Central to our understanding of institutional strength, then, is the institution's *ambition* – the degree to which institutions are designed to change outcomes relative to what they would otherwise be. In Figure 1, this is the distance between the statutory goal (io') and the preinstitutional outcome (po). Some institutions seek to do more than others – raise more taxes, offer greater protection to workers or the environment, more narrowly constrain the executive, or more radically protect private property, for example. Any comparison of the strength of two different institutions must therefore assess not only whether they endure or generate compliance but also how much work they are doing to generate or prevent change.

We might have adopted a relative rather than an absolute concept of institutional strength. In Figure 1 this would mean a focus on the proportion of the institutional goal that is achieved ($S/(io' - po)$ rather than S itself). Although such an approach may be appropriate in some cases (for example, when comparing two identical institutions), it rewards institutions with meager levels of ambition. Institutions that propose to do little and achieve it would appear very strong, while institutions that seek to produce (or prevent) radical transformations and accomplish much, but not all, of their goal would be scored as weaker – even though they are actually doing more work. Thus, an institution can still be relatively strong if it is consequential in terms of its goals, even though it falls short of full compliance. Most of our analysis holds ambition constant and focuses on compliance with and stability of the formal rules. However, we also introduce (below) the concept of "insignificant" institutions to characterize formal rules with no ambition, which do not modify the status quo (po) even when achieving perfect compliance.[11]

---

[11] This does not mean that the level of noncompliance ($io'-io$) is irrelevant. Even an institution that generates significant effects in the direction of its formal goals might pay an important price if compliance is low. The institution may lose legitimacy, and the consequent public cynicism may undermine support for the institution, leading to instability. Scholars have made this argument, for example, in regard to the inclusion of social and economic rights in constitutions of the global South. Although by some measures these institutions have had important effects (Gauri and Brinks 2008; Brinks and Gauri 2013), their uneven application and gaping holes in implementation have led to strong critiques (Mota Ferraz 2010; Langford et al. 2011).

3.1.1 Social Norms and Institutional Strength

This Element focuses on formal institutions.[12] As noted above, however, formal rules always coexist with (unwritten) social norms, or informal institutions, and their effectiveness and stability are often powerfully shaped by their interaction with those norms (see North 1990; Helmke and Levitsky 2004; Levitsky and Ziblatt 2018). Thus, understanding the strength of formal institutions often requires attention to the normative bases of those institutions. This task is simplest in the case of transformative institutions that seek to move outcomes away from a status quo that is congruent with social norms – we can, for example, track movement toward the institutional goal over time. But norms often undergird formal institutions, especially conservative ones. Many formal institutions generate compliance because they are reinforced by strong social norms (Levi 1988, 1997; North 1990).[13] As is always the case when two potential independent variables are colinear, this complicates the empirical exercise of inferring institutional strength. In such a case, to be able to attribute causal efficacy to the formal institution rather than the informal norms, we would want to show that there exists some nontrivial likelihood that the outcome would be different absent the formal institution, in spite of congruent social norms – in other words, that po is distant from the social norms as well. We might find, for example, that some powerful political, social, or economic actor would not be constrained by social norms but is constrained by the formal institution.

When seeking to understand the strength of human rights treaties, for instance, we would be more interested in examining a country that has experienced endemic human rights violations before signing on to the treaty – say, Argentina – than one that has signed many treaties but lacks a recent history of human rights violations (e.g., Costa Rica). (This would be true even if we found that both countries possessed strong social norms that aligned with the values in the human rights treaties.) Similarly, in the case of a conservative institution, we would want to see evidence of substantial pressure for change.

---

[12] Extending the framework in Figure 1 to help us understand the strength of informal institutions would require reconceptualizing po. In the case of a formal institution, the counterfactual po is likely to be the outcome better predicted by existing social norms or the preferences of electoral majorities or dominant societal interests. Thus, norms and other informal institutions are some of the elements that might play a role in establishing the counterfactual against which the formal institution is pushing, along with all the other factors that might produce po. But what is the counterfactual in the absence of a social norm or other informal institution? In many cases, it may be the flip side of what we are discussing here – po for an informal institution might be what the formal institutions would require, or what some powerful actor is seeking to accomplish, or what some combination of interests and strategies would produce.

[13] As Margaret Levi (1988: 52–70; 1997: 19–25) argues, for example, "quasi-voluntary compliance" with tax laws is rooted in social norms or shared expectations of fairness.

Thus, if a reformist government finds that its ambitious policy proposals are repeatedly struck down by the courts – as happened on occasion in post-Pinochet Chile – we might conclude that the constitution is doing more work than if there is no obvious pressure for change.

Many institutions are designed in an effort to bring social norms in line with the institutional goal, effectively making the institution irrelevant over time. This introduces a temporal dimension into the analysis of institutional strength. Perhaps the strongest institutions are those that shape social norms and expectations to the point that they essentially put themselves out of business. Seatbelt laws and antilittering laws appear to have had this effect in some places, creating the possibility that, at least for the short term, the institution could be removed with no consequent change in behavior. Whether those social norms would erode over time without formal institutional reinforcement is an empirical question.

3.1.2 Insignificance

If the strength of an institution is measured by how much difference it makes, then institutions without ambition – where S approaches zero despite full compliance – must be weak. We characterize such institutions as *insignificant*. An institution is insignificant when it simply blesses whatever equilibrium outcome the dominant actors would produce absent the institution. Under conditions of insignificance, everyone complies and the institution is stable, but behavior would be unlikely to change if the institution were taken away. In other words, the institution is superfluous and plays no actual role in guiding the relevant actors' behavior. In the United States, for example, Alabama voters adopted a resolution in 2014 barring the state from adopting foreign laws that were at odds with citizens' existing rights. The primary target was Sharia law, which was unlikely to be adopted in Alabama under any circumstances. The absence of Sharia in Alabama can hardly be attributed to the strength of the institution, nor is it likely that a rash of Sharia legislation is imminent and needs this law to head it off. Despite its symbolic effects for sympathetic anti-Muslim constituents – which we have distinguished as its "policy effects" or the motivations of its creators – the law produces no behavioral effects. A more serious example is Peru's recent ban on mayoral, gubernatorial, and legislative reelection.[14] Given extreme party system fragmentation, electoral volatility, and low public trust, reelection rates were extraordinarily low in Peru during the

---

[14] Mayoral and gubernatorial reelection was banned via legislation in 2015. Legislative reelection was banned via referendum in 2018.

2000s (Weaver 2017). In practice, then, a formal prohibition of incumbent reelection produced little change in behavior or outcomes.

Although institutions sometimes drift into insignificance, many are purposely designed so that S is low. An example is what Brinks and Blass (2013) call "Potemkin Courts." In such cases, constitutional courts are created, and cases decided, according to the letter of the law, but no government is ever seriously constrained by them because judicial preferences and outcomes, by design, match the preferences of dominant political actors. In Peru, for example, President Alberto Fujimori sponsored a set of reforms that ostensibly aimed to strengthen the courts. The 1993 constitution created a Constitutional Tribunal (TC) with many attributes that would have made the Tribunal a strong institutional check on power. But the legislature also passed a law specifying that the votes of six of seven justices – who were named by the legislature – were required to strike down a law. In practice, then, any two of these seven legislatively approved justices could veto a judicial ruling, making it unlikely that any measure the legislative majority truly cared about would be declared unconstitutional. With or without the TC, the Fujimori government's behavior would be essentially the same; the Tribunal's rulings would adapt themselves to the government's preferences and not vice versa.

Some "prior consultation" laws in Latin America may also be characterized as insignificant. Most Latin American states adopted prior consultation laws in the 1990s and early 2000s under external and domestic pressure to implement ILO Convention 169, which calls for mechanisms to consult local indigenous communities prior to the initiation of natural resource extraction projects. In principle, such laws should give local indigenous communities a say over whether or not such projects go forward. In practice, however, prior consultation laws in Mexico, Peru, and elsewhere included no provision for "consulted" indigenous communities to actually stop the projects (Torres Wong 2018: 254). As a result, the outcome of prior consultation is always the same: the projects go forward.[15] This has led some observers to conclude that prior consultation laws are, in effect, insignificant. According to Torres Wong, for example, prior consultation laws "[do] not deter the advancement of extractive industries," even when they are fully complied with (2018: 246, 256–257).[16]

---

[15] According to Torres Wong, "all 66 prior consultation procedures conducted in Bolivia, Mexico, and Peru over hydrocarbon and mining projects resulted in indigenous approval" (2018: 247).

[16] Both Wong (2018) and Eisenstadt et al. (2017) conclude that the main behavioral effect of prior consultation laws is to reduce indigenous mobilization. Falleti (forthcoming), by contrast, argues that in the Bolivian case recently activated prior consultation laws had a significant and positive impact for indigenous communities after the adoption of implementation rules.

Indeed, the actual operation of prior consultation schemes in Latin America runs the gamut from weak to strong and from progressive to conservative, thus usefully illustrating the conceptual points we seek to make here. At the weak end, companies and governments go through empty, pro forma exercises in consultation on projects that have been decided in advance. Full compliance with a weak institution that requires only consultation leads to no discernible change in the outcomes for the companies, the government, or the affected communities. In fact, by channeling conflict into these empty, powerless forums and demobilizing the communities, an ostensibly progressive institution can become a conservative one, making it easier to continue long-standing practices of simply extracting at will from indigenous territories (Rodríguez Garavito 2011: 298–301). In a sense, when this happens the institution is producing a negative S by disempowering its purported beneficiaries. In other cases, prior consultation schemes generate important side payments to affected communities, even when they do not give indigenous communities a meaningful say over whether and how an extractive project will go forward. Here the institution is weak but nevertheless does something. At the other end of the continuum is Colombia, where some communities, under the tutelage of the Constitutional Court, have secured the right to veto particular projects. This occurred, for example, in the case of the expansion of a dam in Embera territory (Rodríguez Garavito 2011: 297; also Thompson 2016: 91; Brinks 2019: 361).

Institutions that are originally insignificant may take on significance if changed circumstances increase S. Such a transformation would, in effect, mirror the process of institutional conversion described by Streeck and Thelen (2005) and Mahoney and Thelen (2010). Yet, unless circumstances happen to move *po* far from its original location, it will often require formal institutional change to make an insignificant institution substantive in terms of its behavioral effects.

Whether an institution designed to be insignificant will endure and be enforced should the day come when actors begin to violate its terms is difficult to know in advance. As Mark Twain once wrote, "the weakest of all weak things is a virtue which has not been tested in the fire."[17] Because the behavior in question is overdetermined, the strength of an insignificant institution is unobservable until circumstances change so that key actors are confronted with a larger S – what if, for instance, the Peruvian legislature had suddenly changed hands (causing *po* to shift) and found itself at odds with a TC appointed by the previous Congress? Such changes often result in pressure for formal

---

[17] Twain puts these words in the mouth of the stranger in "The Man That Corrupted Hadleyburg," a short story that first appeared in *Harper's Monthly* in December 1899.

institutional reform. Argentina's long-established (and long-insignificant) constitutional requirement that presidents be Catholic fell fairly quickly once the non-Catholic population increased and became politically relevant.[18]

Similarly, originally strong institutions can become insignificant over time by shaping preferences to match the institutional goal.[19] The strongest institutions are those that establish new societal norms and achieve compliance by modifying actors' preferences over time. When a rule is so effective that actors internalize it as a norm and compliance becomes taken for granted, its active enforcement may no longer be necessary to achieve behavioral change. In such cases, the formal institution no longer does much work, although this is hardly a sign that the institution was always weak. Rather, the rules have generated a normative change in society that has resulted in essentially voluntary compliance.[20] Here, the evaluation of weakness is a time-bounded one: we might say, then, that the institution was strong enough to produce the outcome and an associated normative change to the point where the institution has become insignificant. In this case, however, the original institution was ambitious and designed to produce significant change. It was its own success rather than a strategic calculation of rule makers that made it insignificant.

3.2 Types of Institutional Weakness

Institutions that are significant on paper – that is, their statutory goals are ambitious, such that $io'\text{-}po > 0$ – may nevertheless fail in distinct ways to achieve those goals. These are forms of institutional weakness. Take, for example, a constitutional amendment that limits presidents to one term. If, before the rule, many presidents enjoyed multiple terms in office and after the rule none do (and *ceteris* is reasonably *paribus*), we can be fairly confident that the institution is strong. There is a great distance between the expected outcome absent the institution, as evidenced by historical events, and that with the institution. An institution is weak, by contrast, when S approaches zero because the rule is ignored. Following the same example, consider Latin American presidents (e.g., Daniel Ortega, Juan Orlando Hernández, Evo Morales) who overstay their term in office despite preexisting constitutional prohibitions. This is one form of weakness,

---

[18] The reform was undertaken during the administration of President Carlos Menem, who had converted from Islam to Catholicism in order to further his political ambition. See www .britannica.com/biography/Carlos-Menem.

[19] Alternatively, an institution may drift into insignificance by not adapting to the context, so that what was originally a demanding standard no longer has any bite (Hacker, 2005; Streeck and Thelen, 2005).

[20] We thank Maria Paula Saffon and Alisha Holland for bringing this point to our attention.

which we will call noncompliance. Here there is no S: the preinstitutional outcome continues to obtain despite the existence and persistence of the rule.

Now consider presidents constrained by term limits who enact a constitutional amendment permitting one or more reelections. When the rules change to suit the preferences of every new actor that comes along, we have the category of weakness we call instability. Take, for instance, the case of Ecuador, where the 2008 constitution – pushed by President Rafael Correa – replaced the ban on reelection with a two-term limit. Correa was reelected in 2009 and 2013.[21] Facing the end of his final term, Correa orchestrated a 2015 referendum that ended term limits for all officials beginning in 2021 – a move that would allow him to run again in 2021. However, his successor – seeking to prevent Correa's return to power – organized another referendum that reestablished term limits. Similarly, the Dominican Republic shifted from indefinite reelection to a ban on immediate reelection in 1994, to a two-term limit in 2002, back to a ban on immediate reelection in 2009, and then back to a two-term limit in 2015.[22] In cases like these, the rules are sequentially changed to match the preferences of successive rule makers. In such cases, rather than forcing preferences to accommodate the institutional outcome, the institution changes to ensure that the outcome matches the preferences of those who were meant to be constrained. In these cases, S disappears through rule changes that lead the institution to match the "preinstitutional" preferences of the key actors.

These two categories of institutional weakness therefore reduce the effective value of S, even for ambitious institutions. Insignificant institutions, by contrast, have a near-zero S despite high levels of compliance and stability. The distinction among these types of weakness is important because, although in each of them S approximates zero, the politics that produce each outcome vary widely. In the section that follows, we discuss institutions that seem significant on paper but are nevertheless weak due to either noncompliance or instability.

3.2.1 Noncompliance

Noncompliance occurs when S should be greater than zero given the rules established by the parchment institutions but the relevant actors, or an important subset of them, are able to disregard the institution rather than comply with or replace it, effectively reducing S to zero. Noncompliance may be rooted in failures at two broad levels: (1) state officials' decision not to enforce, and (2) state officials' incapacity to enforce or elicit societal cooperation.

---

[21] Correa's 2013 reelection already could be seen as a violation of the two-term limit, but he claimed that only post-2008 terms counted under the new constitution.

[22] See Corrales and Penfold (2014: 161).

3.2.1.1 State Nonenforcement

We often assume that state officials will seek to enforce the law – laws, after all, are creations of the state. Frequently, however, noncompliance occurs because state actors choose not to enforce the rules. In these cases, the institution is formally designed to make a difference – it prescribes costly changes in behavior, and the penalties for noncompliance, if applied, are significant – but the relevant state actors simply fail to enforce the rules. An example is what Levitsky and Murillo (2009, 2014) call "window dressing institutions," or institutions that state actors create without any intention of seriously enforcing. Take environmental laws as an example. Brazilian governments adopted an array of environmental regulations in the 1980s and early 1990s, which, on paper, provided Brazil with "unusually strong foundations for environmental law" (Hochstetler and Keck 2007: 51). Through the early 1990s, however, many environmental regulations were not enforced, leading scholars to describe them as "simply a smokescreen for a general abdication of environmental governance" (Hochstetler and Keck 2007: 37). Another example is utility regulation. When cash-strapped Latin American governments privatized public utilities during the 1990s, most of them created independent regulatory agencies in order to enhance investors' confidence (Levi-Faur and Jordana 2006). In practice, however, most of these agencies lacked independent authority and routinely failed to enforce their bylaws (Murillo 2009; Post 2014).

In other cases, executives or legislatures adopt rules with the intention of producing real change, but bureaucrats or local governments in charge of actual enforcement refuse to carry them out. The result is what Alisha Holland (2017) calls forbearance. Holland's study of squatters and street vendors in Chile, Colombia, and Peru, shows that local politicians and bureaucrats with low-income constituencies often deem the human and political costs of enforcing the law to be prohibitively high.

Frequently, state officials will engage in *selective* enforcement, applying the law to certain individuals or groups but not others. The bases for selective enforcement vary, ranging from personal ties (corruption) to partisanship, class, ethnicity, and region. In the post-Reconstruction era US South, for example, suffrage restrictions such as literacy tests and residency requirements were enforced rigorously on African American voters but not poor white voters (Keyssar 2000). For decades in Latin America, anticorruption laws tended to snare either government rivals or officials who were no longer in power, rather than those currently in office (or their associates). And Mexico's 1856 Lerdo Law, which ordered the breakup of all landholdings held by corporate entities in the name of individual property rights, was applied forcefully to Church lands but less rigorously to communally held indigenous lands (Saffon and González Bertomeu, forthcoming). Liberal governments viewed the Church as a political adversary, while indigenous communities were seen as potential allies.

Selective enforcement may be facilitated by institutional design. Laws and regulations sometimes create ambiguities that allow local governments vast discretion in implementation and enforcement – often without technically violating the law (Mahoney and Thelen 2010). For example, Argentina's national antideforestation law granted provincial governments considerable discretion in defining what areas were to be protected and what constituted a violation. As a result, governments varied their enforcement efforts in line with societal pressure; enforcement was lower in provinces where large landowners were most powerful (Fernández Milmanda and Garay forthcoming).[23]

Noncompliance is not always driven by a lack of enforcement. Some institutions establish nonpunitive sanctions for violating what is otherwise a meaningful behavioral restriction. In these cases state actors dutifully impose sanctions for noncompliance, but these sanctions (for example, a minuscule fine) are so low relative to S as to be a meaningless incentive for actors to change their behavior. In effect, the formal rules ensure that the cost of complying significantly exceeds the trivial punishment for noncompliance. For instance, France's 2000 "parity law" required that parties field an equal number of male and female candidates. Parties that failed to comply with the new quotas were forced to pay a moderate-sized fine – one that the larger and wealthier parties were able and willing to pay (Murray 2007: 575). As one conservative party leader put it, "We prefer to pay fines than lose elections!" (quoted in Murray 2007: 571). A similar phenomenon may be observed in Latin America. In El Salvador, Honduras, and Panama, parties may simply pay fines and run male candidates.[24] For all intents and purposes, then, S disappears in these cases because actors behave as if the institution did not exist (except that they pay a trivial penalty). In such a situation, even if enforcement – in the sense of applying sanctions for violations – is 100 percent, the relevant outcome is similar with or without the rule.

---

[23] Fernández Milmanda and Garay show that in the province of Salta, the political influence of landowners led the governor to set a more lenient standard for defining which areas are open to exploitation, as well as low penalties for infractions. Despite this leniency, violators were rarely prosecuted, and consequently 40 percent of deforestation was illegal. Thus, Salta's deforestation law yielded lower compliance relative to its statutory goal than that in Chaco, where local environmentalist groups had more political influence. In fact, Salta's total deforestation nearly doubled Chaco's, even though in both provinces the institution appears to have the same statutory goal (Fernández Milmanda and Garay forthcoming).

[24] https://reformaspoliticas.org/reformas/genero-y-politica/mariana-caminotti/

3.2.1.2 State (In)capacity and Societal Resistance

A different sort of failure occurs when governments possess the will to enforce but lack the capacity to do so relative to societal resistance. This is partly a question of the state's infrastructural power (Mann 1984; Soifer 2015). Some states simply lack the fiscal and administrative capacity to enforce certain laws – particularly ones that seek large-scale behavioral change and require extensive monitoring. For example, governments may not be able to enforce labor, immigration, or environmental laws because the state lacks a sufficient number of trained inspectors or because, due to low public sector salaries or lack of equipment, orders to enforce are simply not carried out on the ground. In some cases, states lack the capacity to even uphold the rule of law (O'Donnell 1993, 1999). As Yashar (2018) shows, for example, the spread of illicit organizations and rising homicide rates in much of contemporary Latin America can be explained, in part, by the sheer weakness of state (i.e., police) monitoring capacities.

Long-run state enforcement capacities are shaped by political choices. As recent work by Schrank (forthcoming) and Amengual and Dargent (forthcoming) shows, levels of enforcement capacity at time t reflect investments in capacity made at t minus x.[25] However, because the development of state capacity takes time (Soifer 2015; Kurtz 2013), and because investments in state capacity may be matched by the growing strength of state challengers (Migdal 1988; Dargent, Feldman, and Luna 2017), it is reasonable to suggest that in some instances, governments possess the will to enforce certain rules but simply lack the infrastructural wherewithal to do so.

We exclude from our analysis failed states that lack even minimal enforcement capacity, focusing on those with at least some infrastructural power but which nevertheless lack the capacity to systematically uphold the law in some areas. These are what Amengual and Dargent (forthcoming) describe as "indifferent" or "standoffish" states.[26] States that can and do enforce some of the rules some of the time but lack the resources to enforce all the rules all of the time. Enforcement is thus *intermittent* in that it does not follow an identifiable pattern, or *selective* in that resource-constrained states target some individuals or groups more than others. As Guillermo O'Donnell (1993) noted in his classic discussion of "brown areas," selective enforcement sometimes follows a territorial logic, with states enforcing the law at a higher rate in the metropolitan centers than in the hinterlands (also Herbst 2000; Soifer 2015). Alternatively, it may

---

[25] Continued low capacity thus calls into question the sincerity of the government's expressed desire to enforce. Indeed, Surnarayan (2016) and Surnarayan and White (2018) show how status inequalities in India and the US South were associated with strategic efforts to weaken state capacity by cross-class coalitions of higher-status individuals.

[26] The term "standoffish state" is taken from Slater and Kim (2015: 30, 39).

follow a class-based logic, in which the wealthier and better-connected members of society evade the reach of a standoffish state, leaving the poor more vulnerable (Brinks 2008; Méndez, O'Donnell, and Pinheiro 1999). The distinction between this and the politically motivated selective enforcement described earlier is not always clear cut. In principle, selectivity in these cases is simply a product of prioritizing resources. In practice, however, a degree of political calculus – state officials' desire to reward supporters, punish rivals, or avoid costly social resistance – invariably weighs in.

In their analysis of the regulatory enforcement in Argentina, Bolivia and Peru, Amengual and Dargent (2018) illustrate how enforcement outcomes vary in standoffish states. In Lima's construction industry, where the local construction chamber actively supported enforcement, government officials cracked down on illegal activities. In Bolivia's gold mining sector, where cooperative miners were political allies of the governing MAS, state officials looked the other way. In the Argentine province of Córdoba, state officials applied labor safety regulations in the construction industry, where union pressure was strong, but ignored flagrant violations in brick-making, where workers were politically and organizationally weak.

As the above examples suggest, the state's will and capacity to enforce are only part of the story. Compliance also depends on the degree of societal cooperation or resistance. Societal responses to institutions vary widely, from active cooperation where the rules align with social norms and power distributions (e.g., property rights laws in the United States) to outright resistance where the rules contradict dominant social norms or are opposed by powerful societal actors. The level of state enforcement effort required to produce compliance will, therefore, be a function of the degree of societal cooperation or resistance. Since enforcement is a costly endeavor for resource-constrained states (Amengual 2016), governments can be expected to tailor enforcement to the degree of expected resistance. Faced with enough resistance, officials may look the other way rather than enforce the law (Amengual and Dargent 2018). As Hochstetler and Keck show, for example, Brazilian antideforestation law is "ample and often well formulated," and the Brazilian state possesses the capacity to enforce it (2007: 51, 151). Because enforcement requires confronting a powerful network of corrupt politicians and criminal organizations, however, governments often exhibit a "lack of desire to expend the necessary political capital and resources to enforce the law" (2007: 151–154). When governments find societal partners that seek and even cooperate with enforcement, however, states are more likely to enforce and will secure similar results with lower effort (Amengual 2016; Amengual and Dargent forthcoming).

The state's enforcement capacity is thus relational.[27] On the one hand, the cost of enforcement can be reduced considerably when, due to the alignment of underlying norms or interests, societal actors cooperate in ensuring compliance – a phenomenon that is sometimes called enforcement "co-production."[28] Where social norms reinforce the rules, "quasi-voluntary" compliance reduces the need for a heavy investment in state enforcement (save occasionally punishing deviant behavior) (Levi 1988: 72–70, 1997: 19–25); indeed, compliance may be high even where state infrastructural power is limited.

On the other hand, when formal rules run up against competing social norms or resistance from powerful interests, greater enforcement effort is necessary to ensure compliance. Strong competing norms or informal institutions – sometimes enforced by nonstate actors such as traditional authorities or religious communities – may inhibit societal cooperation with enforcement (for instance, in reporting of noncompliance) and even create incentives for outright noncompliance (Migdal 1988; Helmke and Levitsky 2004). Where state infrastructural power is limited, the result almost invariably is low compliance. Transformative laws created in pursuit of far-reaching behavioral change in such cases will be limited to "aspirational" status (Htun and Jensenius forthcoming). Sometimes societal resistance is so pervasive that it can overcome almost any enforcement effort, resulting in low compliance despite high state capacity. A classic example is Prohibition in the United States, where a strong state and a substantial investment in enforcement still failed to eliminate the production and consumption of alcohol. Strong institutions, then, are those that produce actual compliance with a demanding standard of behavior. The level of state enforcement effort required to produce that compliance will depend on the degree of societal resistance or cooperation.

In sum, noncompliance is a product of the interplay between state enforcement efforts from above and societal responses from below. If institutions do not change behavior because the relevant state agencies will not or cannot act to compel individuals or firms to follow parchment rules, then S is small with the state's complicity. But compliance may be low even where the state's will and capacity are high. The state may invest considerable resources into enforcing a particular institution, but if societal actors still find ways to continue the proscribed behavior, then the rule is clearly not producing its intended effect.

---

[27] See Migdal (1988); Amengual (2016); Dargent et al (2017).

[28] We take the term from Amengual (2016). Our usage is similar to Levi's concept of quasi-voluntary compliance, in which convergent social norms reduce the cost of monitoring and enforcement, thereby allowing state agents to focus on deviant cases. See also Sabet (2014) and Ostrom (1996). Huber (2007) points to a similar mechanism when he argues that unions reduce the cost of enforcement for Occupational Health and Safety Administration (OSHA) inspectors in the United States.

Strong institutions, then, produce compliance with a demanding standard of behavior when there exists the will and capacity to enforce from above *and* compliance is achieved from below.[29]

3.2.2 Instability

Most variants of institutionalism take a minimum of institutional stability for granted, either because institutions reflect an equilibrium outcome or because they generate positive feedback effects. Indeed, nearly all of our theoretical expectations regarding their effects hinge on the assumption that institutions are minimally stable – that they do not change at each round of the game. And many institutions are designed not so much to produce change as to protect the status quo and extend the preferences of powerful actors into an uncertain future. Institutions can therefore most clearly be seen to "matter" – in the sense of constraining and enabling political actors – when they endure beyond the time in office of those who create them. Otherwise they can be easily dismissed as epiphenomenal. Institutions must, moreover, endure for some time if political actors are to develop the shared expectations and consistent strategies that institutionalist theories lead us to expect.

As Levitsky and Murillo (2009, 2014) have argued, however, institutions vary widely in their "stickiness." In Latin America, one observes instances of extreme institutional instability, or "serial replacement," in which constitutional, electoral, and other key rules of the game are rewritten after virtually every change in government (Levitsky and Murillo 2014). This is the case even with institutions of fundamental importance, such as constitutions. Bolivia, Ecuador, and the Dominican Republic have changed constitutions at an average rate of more than once a decade in the nearly two centuries since independence (Elkins et al. 2009). Latin American electoral systems are also subject to serial replacement; the rate of change in much of the region is considerably higher than in advanced democracies (Remmer 2008; Calvo and Negretto forthcoming). Venezuela employed thirteen different electoral laws between 1958 and 1998 (Crisp and Rey 2001: 176). Ecuador underwent fourteen major electoral reforms between 1980 and 2015 – nearly two major reforms per elected

---

[29] Our focus on compliance does not mean enforcement is irrelevant. As the above discussion of insignificant institutions makes clear, behavior that comports with the institutional goal may not, per se, be evidence of compliance. What looks like compliance might simply mean that the rule does not meaningfully constrain anyone's preferences or possibilities. Behavior in such an instance would be merely correlated with the institutional rules. In these cases, a focus on enforcement can help to identify cases in which the institutional outcome is actually costly to some actors. A large state investment in enforcement is likely to signal a (perceived) large S, even when the absence of noncompliance does not allow us to observe what might happen if the institution did not exist.

president (Calvo and Negretto forthcoming). This pattern is not limited to the federal level. Argentina's twenty-four provinces undertook thirty-four electoral reforms between 1983 and 2003 (Calvo and Micozzi 2005). Institutional stability, then, cannot be taken for granted. Rather, it should be treated as a variable – and another dimension of institutional strength.

We define institutional instability as an excessively high rate of institutional change that leaves political actors unable to develop stable expectations about how the rules work or clear strategies to pursue their interests through them. It seems obvious that institutions that change with every shift in the political winds cannot be called strong. The kind of instability that should be associated with institutional weakness is, however, harder to identify than noncompliance. The problem here is distinguishing instability – an *excessively* high rate of institutional change – from "normal" institutional reform. Sometimes change simply reflects the persistence of the original goals, which requires adaptation to new conditions, such as raising the minimum wage to match inflation; or the aggregate institutional cost might eventually be revealed to be intolerably high, so that the healthy political response would be to amend or replace the institution. Here, institutions are adapting to new information about environmental conditions. Alternatively, environmental conditions and societal power and preference distributions may occasionally vary, generating pressure for reform in even the most institutionally stable environments. Few observers would consider suffrage extension, the adoption of civil service laws, or the adoption of laws legalizing gay marriage in established democracies to be signs of institutional weakness. Rather than institutional instability, these are better thought of as cases of adaptation to changing societal preferences. By contrast, the frequent reinstatement of preexisting rules or a series of reforms with opposing statutory goals are more likely to signal institutional weakness.

Nor is an institution's persistence always a sign of its strength. If S is decreasing over time – say, because inflation is eating away at the minimum wage, as it does in the United States – formal stability could mask a growing weakness. Scholars have labeled this process of institutional change "drift" (Hacker 2005; Streeck and Thelen 2005). For an institution to remain strong in such a context, it must be able to adapt – to undertake reforms that preserve S in the face of changes that threaten the institutional goal. If it maintains S within acceptable and meaningful levels, adaptation may well be a sign of strength. Keeping S as the conceptual touchstone for institutional weakness helps us distinguish adaptation from instability.

Distinguishing between instability and adaptation poses an empirical challenge. The point at which change becomes excessively frequent is a context- and institution-dependent (perhaps even a normatively informed) judgment, which makes comparative analysis difficult. In many cases, measurement will require some kind of counterfactual exercise or the use of comparative benchmarks based on historical rates of institutional change within the country or average rates of change in other countries.

In most contexts, widespread institutional instability is costly, for it narrows time horizons and undermines cooperation in ways that hinder governance and leave democracies vulnerable to abuse, crisis, or both (Levitsky and Murillo 2005; Spiller and Tommasi 2005).[30] Yet polities – even democratic ones – also contain "bad" institutions whose persistence produces harmful effects for important parts of society. Those who are concerned with the negative aspects of the United States' electoral system – from the Electoral College, to gerrymandered districts, to the numerous impediments to registration and suffrage – are understandably frustrated by that country's institutional stability. In some cases, durable institutions also create problems in Latin America. As Albertus and Menaldo (2018) show, many Latin American constitutions maintain key authoritarian features, some of which have proven difficult to replace. Rather than take a normative position with respect to institutional instability, then, we simply seek to identify its occurrence and understand how it affects actors' expectations. Table 1 on the following page summarizes the types of weaknesses we have discussed here.

3.3 Judicial Interpretation as a Source of Noncompliance and Instability

In closing this section, it is worth highlighting one more – often hidden – mechanism that can lead to both noncompliance and instability: judicial (re) interpretation. The judicial power of interpretation is often viewed as a source of institutional strength. Elkins, Ginsburg, and Melton (2009), for example, find that, all other things equal, the existence of a constitutional court with the power of authoritative interpretation considerably extends the life of a constitution. Authoritative interpretation in response to unexpected contingencies and arising exigencies can add needed flexibility to an institutional framework. At the same time, however, judicial interpretations may merely provide "legal" cover and legitimacy for what is clearly a rule violation, or may be manipulated to produce frequent changes in response to changing preferences. Indeed, in contemporary Latin America, powerful actors are increasingly using courts to legitimize noncompliance or instability. This is an important phenomenon. However,

---

[30] For instance, higher levels of political instability have been associated with lower economic growth (Aisen and Veiga 2013), especially in developing countries (Berggen et al. 2012), as well as with lower investment in infrastructure (Henisz 2002).

Table 1: Types of Institutional Weakness

	Type	Description	Examples
Insignificance		Institution has zero ambition, in that it does not prescribe a meaningful change in actors' behavior even when fully enforced and complied with	* *Symbolic institutions;* designed to please an audience but without behavioral effects (e.g., "Potemkin Courts" [Brinks and Blass 2013])
Noncompliance	Type I: Nonenforcement	Institution prescribes significant behavioral change, but state officials choose not to enforce it systematically	* *Window dressing institutions;* created without intent to fully enforce (Levitsky and Murillo 2009)
			* *Forbearance;* strategic neglect of enforcement, usually driven by political incentives (Holland 2017)
			* *Selective enforcement;* state officials vary in enforcement across territory or across different societal groups
	Type II: Nonpunitive enforcement	Rule is enforced and sanctions are applied, but the sanctions are too weak to change behavior	* *Unsanctioned institutions;* strategically designed to be enforced without effect due to trivial penalties

Type III: Weak State Capacity Relative to Societal Resistance	Government officials seek compliance with the institution but lack sufficient state capacity or societal cooperation to systematically enforce it	* *Standoffish states;* intermittent enforcement following path of least societal resistance (Amengual and Dargent forthcoming) * *Aspirational laws;* created with expectation of low societal compliance but with goal of long-term change in social norms (Htun and Jensenius forthcoming)
Instability	Rules change at an unusually high rate and in contradictory directions, preventing actors from developing stable expectations around them	* *Serial replacement;* rules and procedures are replaced wholesale, without ever becoming entrenched or settling into a stable equilibrium (Levitsky and Murillo 2014)

because judicial interpretation is simply an alternative means of generating rule changes (i.e., instability) or noncompliance, we do not consider it a separate category of institutional weakness.

Perhaps the most prominent example of weakness through judicial interpretation has been in the context of presidential efforts to circumvent constitutional term limits. Under Alberto Fujimori, for instance, Peru's Congress passed an "authentic interpretation" of the two-term limit imposed by the 1993 Constitution, allowing Fujimori to seek a third term in 2000 on the grounds that his first term began under the old constitution. Although most legal experts deemed that interpretation to be in blatant violation of the "true" meaning of the constitution, Peru's Constitutional Tribunal allowed it to stand. Peru is not alone in this respect. In other cases, Supreme Courts (Nicaragua and Honduras) or Constitutional Tribunals (Bolivia) enabled powerful presidential efforts to circumvent constitutional term limits via dubious rulings that interpreted term limits as a violation of a "higher" constitutional right to run for office. In these cases, then, judicial interpretations of the law by friendly (if not subordinate) courts allowed presidents to circumvent the law.

Whether interpretive claims by the courts are merely cover for noncompliance and instability on the one hand or instances of legitimate adaptability and flexibility on the other can be difficult to determine. As in the case of the impeachments chronicled by Helmke (2017, forthcoming), it is not always clear whether the use of a norm or interpretation to justify behavior is pretextual or legitimate. Nevertheless, we can identify some reliable indicators of weakness. These include (1) frequent flip-flops on the part of the court on the meaning of a provision, especially if they are clearly motivated by partisan sympathies; (2) a broad-based consensus on the part of legal or other experts that the interpretation lacks technical merit; (3) an all-too-evident pattern of interpretations that respond to the interests of powerful actors; and (4) interpretations that do not outlive the tenures of the judges who produce them. Some cases will be more obvious than others, but in each case, it will be the researcher's task to persuade the audience that a court is complicit in the production of institutional weakness.

4 Accounting for Institutional Weakness

This section examines the origins of institutional weakness; the following section will undertake a more concrete discussion, grounded in these abstract guidelines, of the origins of institutional weakness in Latin America. We propose some initial hypotheses to account for the different types of institutional weakness we identified in the previous section. In our characterization of institutional strength, S is the cost of the institution to the actors who prefer what we call the preinstitutional outcome (*po*, in Figure 1) – that is, the outcome absent the institution, or under a different preferred institutional arrangement. Although we do not deny the role of other factors – such as voluntary compliance rooted in social norms – in generating institutional strength, our theory is, at its core, a coalitional one, in that it centers on political support for the institution and its enforcement. For the sake of simplicity, we assume that for every institution, there exists one coalition of actors that supports it and another coalition of actors that prefers an alternative outcome. Actors who oppose a particular institution have three options: (1) comply at cost S, (2) avoid compliance and face the cost of a violation (V),[31] or (3) change the institution at cost C to achieve a new S. This formulation suggests that there may well be tradeoffs between noncompliance and instability.

An institution is strong if the cost for opponents of either changing it (C) or violating it (V) exceeds S, the cost of the institutional outcome. Typically, this will depend on the capacity of institutional supporters to block change *and* produce enforcement. Institutions are weak, on the other hand, when the cost of either changing or violating them is lower than S, the cost of compliance, so that either or both options (2) and (3) are on the table. To explain institutional weakness we need to understand what factors raise and lower the cost of V and C relative to S and relative to each other. That is, we expect institutions to be stable and regularly complied with when the cost of changing the institution (C) is higher than the cost imposed by the institution (S) or the cost of a violation (V). Conversely, noncompliance should be high when the cost of violating (V) is lower than the cost imposed by the institution (S) or the cost of replacing it (C). Instability should be high when replacing the rule (C) is cheaper than accepting its cost (S) or the cost of sanctions for violating it (V). To identify the source of institutional weakness, then, we should examine the conditions that shape the value of complying with a particular institution (S), vis-à-vis either changing it (C) or violating it (V).

4.1 Sources of (Non)compliance

One important dimension of institutional weakness is noncompliance: institutions set out ambitious goals but fail to make a difference because actors do not comply with them. As a result, an S that is large on paper can be

---

[31] V, of course, is a function of both the magnitude of the penalty for a violation and the probability of facing the sanction.

dramatically reduced in practice. We argued above that institutional compliance might be undermined due to a lack of meaningful enforcement effort, a lack of enforcement capacity relative to societal resistance, and nonpunitive sanctions. Here we briefly examine some potential sources of these failures.

4.1.1 Strategic Adoption of Weak Institutions

Noncompliance may be associated with limited enforcement efforts by state actors. Some institutions are weak because state officials simply lack an interest in enforcing them. Political actors may even purposely design formal institutions that predictably produce little or no behavioral change because they do not plan to enforce them; or they create institutions with trivial sanctions and enforce them in ways that do not produce the required change in behavior. Why would governments create (or maintain) an institution if they do not actually seek to produce the ostensible goal? Why would politicians incur the cost (in terms of time and political capital) of designing institutions that generate no real-world effects? An answer lies in the *audience value* generated by institutional reforms.

International norm diffusion, reinforced by transnational advocacy networks (Keck and Sikkink 1998) and international organizations such as the World Bank, IMF, and the UN, led many lower- and middle-income governments to perceive a high return on certain institutional reforms (Dobbins, Simmons, and Garrett, 2007; Henisz, Bennet, and Guillen 2005). Governments often claim credit with domestic or international audiences for a substantive achievement when they have done nothing more than create a window dressing institution – one that is intended to be toothless. In particular, a window dressing institution may be a preemptive move to reduce pressure for real change from external actors – often international, but also domestic in the case of subnational actors or particular interest groups. Thus, the audience value, in terms of international prestige, external support, pleasing federal authorities, or sustaining the good will of religious and other domestic cultural elites, outweighs the cost of institutional design, turning C into a net benefit rather than a cost.

In short, window dressing institutions are created by governments seeking to secure the legitimacy gains of adopting an institutional reform without incurring more than a trivial S. The government might claim to have taken action to fight corruption or global climate change or to advance the cause of human, indigenous, or women's rights, even though it only passes a law that effects no meaningful change. In this scenario, rule writers do not seek to depart from the preinstitutional outcome but nevertheless derive some benefit from the mere act of institutional creation. When audience value turns C into a net benefit, governments that prefer the status quo have an incentive to design ostensibly transformative institutions with the full expectation that they will have no real-world effect.[32]

There are, however, different ways of avoiding S. Where V is low, governments seeking audience benefits without altering the status quo frequently design window dressing institutions, or institutions they have no intention of enforcing. During the 1990s and early 2000s, for example, many Latin American governments responded to international pressure by adopting anticorruption laws, judicial reforms, or statutes to protect human rights, women's rights, or indigenous rights. In many of these cases, the costs of actual compliance were quite high – either for governments themselves (anticorruption laws) or for powerful private actors (e.g., environmental regulation). In reality, however, designers often had no intention of incurring the cost of enforcing or complying with them in practice. Rather, they could claim credit for an institution without actually confronting S, the cost of compliance. This is possible when the primary audience – members of the international community, for example – lacks the monitoring capacity to reliably observe violations. An example of rules adopted to please international and domestic audiences is regulations on prior consultation based on ILO Convention 169 of 1989. Fifteen of twenty-two countries that ratified that convention are in Latin America (Falleti and Riofrancos 2018: 89). In Bolivia, ILO 169 and subsequent regulations governing prior consultation of indigenous communities have been more often weak than strong. Adopted in 1991 in response to large scale mobilization by the Indigenous Confederation of the Eastern, Chaco, and Amazonia of Bolivia (CIDOB), these institutions were, at least initially, "designed to not be enforced or complied with" (Falleti forthcoming).[33]

By the same logic, governments may choose to leave weak institutions on the books, if the act of removing them would generate significant audience costs. Such costs could come, for instance, in the form of an outcry (and possible withdrawal of support) from influential international or domestic actors. An example is antiabortion laws. Although abortion bans have rarely been enforced in South America, moves to legalize abortion predictably

---

[32] Designers may be surprised later on, when these institutions are activated and begin producing important effects. Proponents of the institutional goal might be able to put together an enforcement coalition without incurring the cost of replacing or reforming existing rules. In fact, this may be the intended strategy, as we will see below in the discussion of aspirational rules.

[33] Governed by a single article in Bolivia's 1992 Law 1333 on the environment, consultations with indigenous communities were only sporadically undertaken during the 1990s (Falleti and Riofrancos 2018: 100).

trigger intense opposition from the Catholic Church.[34] Similarly, divorce was banned in Argentina until 1987 and in Chile until 2008 despite widespread *de facto* marital dissolution. According to Htun (2003), these laws were designed (and retained) primarily to achieve moral or symbolic goals rather than to actually shape behavior. In many countries, laws prohibiting marijuana consumption have a similar window dressing status. Hence, just as the creation of window dressing institutions may yield political benefits, removing weak institutions from the books may be politically costly, inducing powerful actors to simply deactivate the rule by ignoring its enforcement. In this case, then, the endurance of a weak institution is a strategy to avoid the political cost of what is, at some level, simply a move to align institutions with behavior.

Not all predictably weak institutions are the product of a cynical political exercise. Occasionally, political actors design rules that are unlikely to be complied with today in the hope that they will be complied with in the future. Rule writers may understand (or fear) that in the near term, institutional opponents will be able to avoid enforcement, perhaps because the institution competes with existing social norms or informal institutions or because they are aware of their weak political influence beyond the moment of rule writing. In these cases, the contemplated S may be substantial, but the cost of violations is limited by some combination of low enforcement capacity and limited societal coproduction. In effect, champions of the institutions bet on the future, hoping that changing conditions will permit increased enforcement, or "activation," of the rules in some future round. Htun and Jensenius (forthcoming) label these *aspirational* laws. Examples of aspirational laws include many of the social rights in Brazil's 1988 constitution (Gauri and Brinks 2008) and other recent Latin American constitutions and, as Htun and Jensenius show, laws against domestic violence in Mexico. According to Htun and Jensenius, "aspirational laws," such as Mexico's 2007 Law on Women's Access to a Life Free from Violence are passed in full knowledge that they will not change behavior in the short term but nevertheless seek to establish "goal posts, stakes in future developments, and guides to the process of social change."

In these cases, at the time of institutional creation, supporters may trade a weak enforcement regime for a strong substantive rule. The easiest compromise with opponents may be one in which the potential S is quite large, but V is

---

[34] It is worth noting that even unenforced antiabortion laws generate distributive effects, as shown by the experience of Argentina. Uneven access to public services in the permitted cases of rape and maternal health risks, along with rates of complications due to clandestine abortions, vary by social class and province, helping to explain the unsuccessful 2018 mobilization to replace the law and legalize abortion.

kept low through weak enforcement – with the expectation that V will grow in the future through investment in enforcement resources or changes in social norms, which do not require a complex process of institutional creation.

Aspirational laws may be activated – made effective through enforcement rather than formal institutional change – when the coalition supporting the institution strengthens, such that it either gains control of enforcement or exerts greater influence over those who control it. In 2005, Bolivia elected its first indigenous president. Not only did Morales' Movement Toward Socialism (MAS) receive an outright majority of the vote in a previously fragmented party system, but the support of the indigenous movement was crucial for its electoral success (Madrid 2012; Anria 2013). Once in power, the MAS coalition approved the 2005 Hydrocarbon Law, which allowed for the actual implementation of a prior consultation system that, though formally established when Bolivia ratified the ILO 169 convention in 1991, had previously been limited to parchment. The 2005 law made prior consultation mandatory and binding for hydrocarbon projects (Falleti and Riofrancos 2018: 101). In effect, then, the MAS's rise to power triggered the activation of what had previously been a window dressing institution. Likewise, in the United States, the right to vote regardless of race was enshrined in the Fifteenth Amendment to the Constitution in 1870 but was unenforced, or actively denied, in much of the country for nearly a century. This constitutional right was not activated until demographic and political changes in the African American community gave rise to a powerful civil rights movement that, acting in tandem with the courts, produced a coalition capable of generating compliance.

As the above example suggests, institutional activation may be driven, in part, by judicial interpretation. Courts across Latin America have activated social rights provisions in their constitutions, which had previously been ignored in practice (Langford 2008; Gauri and Brinks 2008). Colombia is probably the best example of the activation of constitutional rights through vigorous and expansive constitutional interpretation. For example, Colombia's Constitutional Court essentially rewrote that country's Civil Code to eliminate gender discriminatory provisions in line with prevailing norms of gender equality, first between men and women (Oquendo 2006), but eventually opening a path for the legalization of same-sex marriage (Landau 2017: 232–235).

4.1.1.1 Implementation and Enforcement Gaps

A second source of weak enforcement is a disjuncture between rule writers and rule enforcers and other power holders (i.e., those with the power to affect compliance on the ground). Whereas scholarship on bureaucracies in advanced democracies draws attention to the phenomenon of bureaucratic shirking when the preferences of rule writers and enforcers do not coincide, the degrees of freedom in this gap are usually constrained by the statutory goals of the parchment rule.[35] In weak institutional contexts, by contrast, rule writers do not necessarily constrain enforcers, even where parchment laws prescribe such control. In practice, the coalition in control of the rule-writing process (legislators, constituent assembly members, technocrats in the executive) may not control key agencies of enforcement, such as local governments, bureaucracies, courts, and the security forces, allowing them to have greater degrees of freedom in deciding whether to enforce or not.

Diverging preferences over design and enforcement can often be especially pronounced in hybrid or transitional regimes in which elected officials do not fully control the state. Take, for example, hybrid regimes in which civilian governments exercise little control over the security forces. Governments may adopt human rights laws that the security forces do not comply with (e.g., Guatemala in the 1980s). Or consider cases in which nominally independent constituent assemblies or legislatures exercise little real power over executives (who, in most instances, control prosecutors, the police, and the armed forces) and thus design laws that they cannot make binding. For example, Mexico's 1917 constitution – drawn up by a relatively independent convention during the Mexican Revolution – was "one of the most radical of its time" (Knight 1986: 470), but the more moderate President Venustiano Carranza, who controlled the revolutionary army, ignored its most radical clauses (Wilkie 1967: 56).

Even in democracies, multiple levels of government and fragmented bureaucracies and security forces may hinder enforcement of laws and rules that national governments seek to enforce. Thus, where state capacity is uneven across the national territory (O'Donnell 1993, 1999), decentralization may weaken some institutions. If enforcement is entrusted to multiple levels of government, with different constituencies shaping their preferences, certain institutions may be vulnerable to local-level "forbearance" – a dynamic that O'Donnell (1999, 2004) highlighted in his discussion of "brown areas."

---

[35] See Huber and Shipan (2002) and Carpenter (2001) for summaries and arguments about these processes in the rational choice and historical institutionalist traditions, respectively. Mahoney and Thelen (2010) also point to gaps in compliance based on divergent interpretations between rule writers and enforcers as a source of hidden change that keeps institutional structures intact while modifying statutory effects. Whereas in their view, the gap is limited by the degree of discretion established by the existing rules, in our perspective the options are broadened by the possibility of ignoring enforcement or applying it selectively beyond what is written in parchment regulations.

Disjunctures between distinct levels of government may also occur when the designers of national-level institutions hold preferences that differ markedly from those of local officials charged with enforcing them. As Holland (forthcoming) points out, there is often a greater public appetite for rules that require some desired behavior than for the difficult work and painful choices involved in imposing sanctions for their violation. Whereas the general public, which is remote from the site of noncompliance, often prefers a large S, at least in the abstract, state officials who are closer to the targets of a regulatory scheme may be deterred by the social or political cost of enforcement. Thus, national legislatures may pass broadly popular laws against squatting or street vending, but local governments and bureaucrats operating at the site of non-compliance are often reluctant to impose the costs that are required to actually change behavior (Holland, forthcoming). Mayors whose constituents would lose their homes or livelihoods if regulations were enforced, or local bureaucrats who actually oversee enforcement, are thus likely to hold preferences over enforcement that diverge markedly from the national officials who design the laws. The result is a "coercion gap," in which laws are written and passed by national officials but not enforced by local ones.

Fernández Milmanda and Garay's (forthcoming) analysis of deforestation in the Argentine Chaco also points to conflicting views of enforcement between different levels of government. The 2007 Native Forest Protection Regime (NFPR) was spearheaded by national legislators with an environmentalist bent whose urban constituents stood to lose very little under new laws restricting deforestation in the Chaco region. By contrast, provincial governors from the region, who were responsible for enforcing new environmental regulations, had to deal with powerful agricultural producers who had much to lose and were an important part of their constituencies, which raised the cost of enforcement for them.

A disjuncture between rule writers and power holders may also emerge in democracies that coexist with high socioeconomic inequality. Democracy shifts rule-writing power further down the socioeconomic ladder (the median voter is likely to be well below the mean income), and in cases of extreme inequality, the median income earner is poor. If the burden of a particular institution lands primarily on the rich, wealthy individuals may well possess sufficient resources to lobby against enforcement structures, buy off the enforcers – for example, local mayors and judges – and otherwise prevent full enforcement. For such individuals, the real cost of V is reduced even though the rules on the books are nominally universal (Lieberman 2003; Brinks and Botero 2014). Additionally, inequality usually allows the rich to exert disproportionate influence at the design stage (in the executive branch or the legislature), leaving the poor with few options other than protesting at the site of implementation. Thus, social inequality may exacerbate preference gaps between design and enforcement.

4.1.2 State Capacity and Societal Resistance

Nonenforcement is often attributed to state weakness. Rules are violated because state officials lack the skills and resources necessary to enforce them. But this structuralist view – state capacity is a slow-moving variable rooted in long-term historical processes (Centeno 2002; O'Donnell 1999; Soifer 2015) – obscures a more complex (and politically interesting) reality. Most Latin American states possess at least a modest capacity to enforce laws. Indeed, even seemingly weak state agencies have at times demonstrated striking enforcement capacity: Mexico's nineteenth-century state was capable of seizing and breaking up church properties in the name of liberal property rights (Saffon and Gonzáles Bertomeu forthcoming); the Dominican state proved capable of enforcing labor regulations (Schrank, 2013, 2018); some Latin American mayors proved capable of cracking down on squatting and street vending (Holland 2017); and local governments in crime-ridden cites like Santa Tecla, El Salvador; Medellín, Colombia; Ciudad Juárez, Mexico; and Rio de Janeiro, Brazil have at times dramatically reduced violence (WOLA 2011; Moncada 2016). Hence, we view institutional enforcement efforts as driven as much by political choices as by underlying state capacity. Indeed, there is simply too much variation in enforcement in Latin America – within states over time, or across comparably weak states – to ignore the role of political decisions in either the short or the long term.

Over the long run, weak state enforcement capacity is at least partly a product of past political decisions not to invest in building state capacity. It takes time to build state capacity (Kurtz 2013; Soifer 2015), and states that fail to do the work of enforcing a certain regulatory framework over time often find it difficult to suddenly generate compliance when the government's preferences change. New enforcement efforts run up against the established expectations of both state and social agents. Yet enforcement capacity can be built – and sometimes quite rapidly. For example, Colombia's Constitutional Court was strong almost immediately after it was established in 1992 (Cepeda Espinoza 2004). This outcome defied longstanding expectations in the comparative judicial politics literature about the requisite maturation time for new courts (Carrubba 2009; Epstein, Knight, and Shvetsova 2001), as well as Colombia's reputation as a weak state. Likewise, Peruvian technocrats – operating in a notoriously weak state – created effective economic policy-making institutions within the Finance Ministry under President Alberto Fujimori (Dargent 2015); and as Andrew Schrank (forthcoming), shows, the Dominican government – facing the threat of US trade sanctions – introduced a set of Weberian administrative reforms that quickly gave rise to a more effective labor inspectorate during the 1990s.

But if enforcement is possible in weaker states, it is nevertheless costly. The sheer logistical requirements of monitoring consume vast resources; and enforcement may trigger resistance from powerful actors or electorally consequential constituencies. Holland (2017, forthcoming) highlights the importance of what might be called sanction aversion, or the underenforcement that can result from state officials' calculation that the social or political costs of enforcement outweigh its benefits. Where public sector resources and political capital are scarce, then, governments that possess the raw capacity to enforce laws may nevertheless opt for strategic forbearance or the selective use of enforcement, following what is, in effect, the path of least resistance. According to Amengual and Dargent (forthcoming), the latter strategy is followed by "standoffish states." Standoffish states can – and sometimes do – enforce the law. But because enforcement requires costly investments of scarce resources and political capital, governments are only likely to take action when significant countervailing constituencies mobilize behind the effort (Amengual 2016; Dargent et al. 2017; Amengual and Dargent forthcoming). Standoffish behavior is particularly likely in unequal democracies, where the rich (but also, as Holland shows, the poor) possess a range of tools with which to resist enforcement efforts. Sometimes opponents do not bother to mobilize to block the passage of particular laws, counting instead on being able to neutralize them at the time of application.

"Standoffish states" are widespread in Latin America. The region's unequal democracies frequently give rise to ambitious institutional reforms aimed at regulating the powerful or protecting the vulnerable. These reforms are often designed by a handful of state actors operating without strong societal coalitions. Thus, efforts to generate compliance often confront fierce resistance on the ground. Without societal support, systematic enforcement requires a vast expenditure of human and financial resources, which are hardly abundant in most Latin American states.

Although the state's default strategy is often nonenforcement (Amengual and Dargent forthcoming), standoffish states may enforce the law when societal mobilization creates incentives for them to do so. In Bolivia, social mobilization led to unprecedented enforcement of prior consultation laws in the 2000s (Falleti forthcoming). In Brazil, where extensive environmental legislation had been on the books since the 1960s but was largely unenforced, the mobilization of environmental activist networks led to greater (if still intermittent) state enforcement efforts in the 1980s and 1990s

(Hochstetler and Keck 2007). Likewise, in the Argentine city of Rosario, where environmental regulations were routinely unenforced during the early twenty-first century, allowing the Santa Clara plant to pollute the local air and water with impunity, mobilization by community organizations such as the *Vecinal Santa Teresita* – together with allies in the municipal government – generated public pressure on the provincial government to enforce the law (Amengual and Dargent, forthcoming).

In some cases, the activation of weakly enforced institutions is driven by long-term changes in underlying power distributions. Mexico's *Lerdo Law*, which was passed under Benito Juarez's liberal government, was initially ignored by the courts, which deferred to long-established norms protecting collective property rights of indigenous communities. This changed during the late-nineteenth-century export boom, which increased the value of commercial land. As the distribution of power shifted toward agricultural exporters, the courts developed a preference for the once-dormant Juarez-era law. Thus, individual property rights laws that had long been selectively enforced on the Church but not indigenous communities were activated via court rulings during the *Porfiriato*. Hence, during the *Porfiriato*, booming export markets and the rising power of local landowners strengthened incentives for enforcement, which resulted in the large-scale breakup of communally owned indigenous lands (Saffon and González Bertomeu forthcoming).

International actors may strengthen pro-enforcement coalitions (Keck and Sikkink 1998; Hochstetler and Keck 2007). As Schrank's (forthcoming) study of Dominican labor inspectors shows, the US government's decision to allow unions and other nongovernmental organizations to petition the United States Trade Representative on behalf of Dominican workers "externalized the costs" of monitoring the country's new labor standards and, by raising the specter of a loss of trade preferences due to noncompliance, created powerful new incentives for the Dominican state to invest in enforcement capacity.

4.1.3 Societal Sources of Compliance

As noted above, the state's enforcement capacity is relational. Some institutions fail to achieve widespread compliance even though governments possess both the will and what appears to be a reasonable capacity to enforce them. These are often institutions that compete with preexisting societal norms and/or are difficult to monitor. Examples include prohibition laws in the United States, labor and environmental regulations in much of Latin America (Amengual 2016), and laws regulating violence against women in Mexico (Htun and Jensenius forthcoming). In such cases, state enforcement requires societal cooperation. Without societal partners to engage in self-reporting or monitoring on the ground, and thus to "mobilize and push an indifferent bureaucracy to action" (Amengual and Dargent forthcoming), compliance may remain low despite state officials' enforcement capacity.

For example, as Hochstetler and Keck (2007: 37, 234) show, much of the environmental regulation adopted by Brazilian governments in the 1980s was "window dressing" aimed in part at pleasing international audiences. Activation of these laws "required a much longer – and protracted – struggle" by networks of local environmental groups. Civil society mobilization, together with judicial intervention, was essential to create the "lateral support" necessary for the effective application of Brazil's environmental laws (Brinks and Botero 2014; Hochstetler and Keck 2007). Another example is efforts to regulate the Santa Clara plant in Rosario, Argentina (Amengual and Dargent forthcoming). Not only did mobilization by community and environmental groups compel the provincial government to abandon its standoffish attitude toward Santa Clara's pollution, but these groups also worked actively with provincial regulators to beef up monitoring of Santa Clara. Local activists and city council members formed a Monitoring Committee – which included provincial regulators and even plant managers – that reinforced state monitoring efforts and served as a source of political pressure on the regulators and the firm. Societal coproduction may yield high levels of compliance even where states are quite weak. In Colombia, for example, the cooperation of local business interests enabled mayors in cities like Bogota and Medellín to successfully implement participatory policies aimed at reducing criminal violence (Moncada 2016).

Enforcement is often most challenging when institutions seek to change deeply ingrained social norms and behavior patterns. Thus, in their study of laws against domestic violence in Mexico, Htun and Jensenius (forthcoming) found that the law was resisted not only by its targets – the abusers – but also by its purported beneficiaries. Their analysis of survey results suggests that many women do not report domestic violence because doing so runs counter to existing norms (which treat domestic violence as a private, family matter). Others opt not to report out of fear of the potential costs of reporting, including material privation (for example, where abusers are breadwinners and are removed from the home) or retaliation. Thus, both competing social norms and material interests may reinforce the behavior that domestic violence laws seek to proscribe. Such bottom-up resistance on the part of beneficiaries clearly robs the institution of the potential for societal coproduction.

Similarly, Tulia Falleti (forthcoming) argues that for new institutions to achieve compliance in a context of state weakness, they must gain broad legitimacy, which may be achieved through the political incorporation of the affected groups. When an institution's beneficiaries become an important part of the political ecosystem – through direct participation or as a support base for institutional designers – it is more likely that governments will invest in enforcement and that societal actors will cooperate. Thus, in her analysis of mechanisms of prior consultation with indigenous communities in Bolivia's hydrocarbons sector, Falleti argues that these institutions were eventually activated when the MAS government of Evo Morales endowed them with greater legitimacy. Because the MAS had politically incorporated indigenous communities, MAS-sponsored institutions of prior consultation were broadly accepted and complied with by all parties in the hydrocarbon sector.

4.2 Sources of Insignificance: Audience Costs and Preemptive Design

Institutions, as noted earlier, are insignificant when they generate outcomes that simply mirror what would happen in the institution's absence. Insignificant institutions differ from the window dressing institutions described above in that they actually appear to generate compliance, but their presence does little or nothing to change behavior on the ground. Why would rule makers design institutions that neither change the status quo nor address any significant challenges to it? As in the case of window dressing institutions, the incentive to create these institutions lies in audience values that turn C into a benefit rather than a cost. External or domestic actors may demand the adoption of laws or regulations resisted by rule makers or powerful stakeholders, leading rule makers to create purely symbolic responses with high audience value. But in these cases, the cost of a blatant violation is high, which precludes the adoption of window dressing institutions. As an alternative, state officials may design rules that, while maintaining an outward appearance of significance, render the institution toothless in its effects. An example is the creation of "Potemkin courts" – constitutional arrangements that create seemingly independent Constitutional Courts to satisfy international donors but which include "poison pill" mechanisms that enable executives to control them or limit their effectiveness without actually violating the formal rules (Brinks and Blass 2013). Attacks on high courts are very visible, even to outside audiences, and they carry high reputational costs – the foreign audience, in a sense, is part of the enforcement regime. When the fine print of the rules themselves produces a weak or subservient court, however, it is much more difficult to muster the requisite outrage in the international community. In these cases, the courts do not impose a significant cost on incumbent governments, even when everyone plays by the rules, and they can actually legitimize behavior of dubious constitutionality. Thus, the cost of the institution is intentionally kept low by the designers because the cost of a violation is expected to be high.

4.3 Sources of Instability

What accounts for institutional instability? As noted above, we expect institutional instability where, for those in a position to craft new institutions, the cost of change (C) is consistently lower than both the cost of accepting the institutional outcome (S) *and* the cost of violating the institution (V). Endemic institutional instability like we observe in much of Latin America suggests that key actors must frequently find S to be unacceptably high, or they must routinely find the cost of replacement to be very low – or both.

4.3.1 Economic Instability

One source of institutional instability is a high frequency of economic shocks. Pressure for institutional change emerges when an environmental change alters S, which is more likely in regions that, due to nondiversified economies and dependence on natural resources and external financing, are more exposed to economic shocks.[36] Thus, an economic crisis that erodes public support for existing policy arrangements, such as that which occurred in Argentina in 2001–2002, may lead elected officials to conclude that the cost of leaving those arrangements intact (S) is unacceptably high. Or a prolonged commodities boom could lead now-popular presidents to view the cost of constitutional term limits (S) as unacceptably high. In short, whenever an exogenous change suddenly and dramatically increases S, such that it exceeds the cost of replacement, we can expect pressure for institutional change.

For instance, in their analysis of the instability of electoral institutions in Latin America, Calvo and Negretto (forthcoming) argue that economic shocks increase public discontent with the status quo and create electoral constituencies for institutional reform. Where economic performance is poor or unstable, citizens will be less attached to existing rules of the game and thus less inclined to defend the institutional status quo. Likewise, Albertus and Menaldo (2018) find that economic crises increase the likelihood that authoritarian holdover constitutions will be dismantled. Similarly, Henisz and Zelner (2005) point to

---

[36] Campello and Zucco (2016) suggest that dependence on commodities and foreign capital increased political swings on presidential popularity, which, in turn, can generate electoral volatility. Indeed, Remmer (1991) and Murillo and Visconti (2017) find that, in Latin America, negative economic shocks increase electoral volatility and anti-incumbent vote. Van de Walle (2001) finds that economic crisis brought about institutional experimentation (often of the window dressing kind) to Africa in the 1990s.

the impact of negative economic shocks on the survival of regulatory agreements in the Argentine and Indonesian electricity sectors. They argue that economic crises raise salience and allow coalitions opposed to existing regulatory frameworks to gain new allies through social justice frames that highlight an unfair distribution of economic pain.

4.3.2 Unstable Coalitions

Another reason why institutions may be unstable is that the coalitions underlying them are fluid. In other words, those who design the rules are often not around to sustain them, as they are soon replaced by actors with different institutional preferences. That is, another source of institutional instability is what might be called actor volatility, or a high frequency of change in the rule writers and the coalitions behind particular institutions. Perhaps those who bear the cost of S (and who may have been the losers in the last round of institution making) are now in a position to change the institution. In this case, instability is not so much a function of a change in outside circumstances but rather of changes in the preferences of the institution-makers. When it is politics that is unstable, so that competing coalitions with divergent preferences frequently alternate in power, we expect institutional replacement to alternately reduce and increase S, as different actors accede to power and pursue different institutional objectives through institutional change.

Frequent turnover in power – from soldiers to civilians, from leftists to rightists, from populists to antipopulists – should increase the frequency of institutional reform attempts, particularly when turnover yields far-reaching change in the preferences of rule-writing coalitions. So, too, should extreme electoral volatility, in which political actors rise and fall quickly, with outsiders often ascending quickly to power and incumbent "insiders" declining rapidly and even disappearing from the political scene. There is some evidence that outsider coalitions are more likely to try to rewrite the rules when they win power (Weyland 2002). And when the coalition behind the old rules collapses and disappears, fewer actors will remain to defend them, leaving the institutional status quo highly vulnerable.

Calvo and Negretto (forthcoming), for example, find that electoral volatility is a major determinant of electoral rule change. There appear to be two reasons for this. First, parties seek to rewrite the rules whenever doing so would improve their electoral standing. Where electoral volatility is low, such that each party's share of the electorate remains relatively stable, parties will see fewer advantages in rule changes. By contrast, where parties' electoral fortunes change quickly and dramatically, politicians will rethink the rules with greater frequency. According to Calvo and Negretto (forthcoming), the rate of electoral reform is higher in Latin American countries with historically high levels of electoral volatility (such as Ecuador) than in countries with low electoral volatility (such as Honduras and Paraguay).

Electoral volatility also encourages institutional instability by undermining the coalitions that create and sustain the rules. In a context of extreme volatility, the partisan composition of governments and legislatures often changes dramatically. Dominant parties decline rapidly and even disappear, while new ones emerge out of nowhere and become dominant (e.g., Peru and Venezuela in the 1990s). The collapse of the coalitions that designed the rules and the ascent of new actors with no stake in the existing ones increase the likelihood of rule changes. For example, Ecuador's 1998 constitution was designed by a coalition that included established progressive parties and a then-powerful indigenous movement (De La Torre 2010). Soon after the constitution was approved, however, the existing parties collapsed and the indigenous movement divided and weakened. This permitted the 2006 election of outsider Rafael Correa, who ran in opposition to the established parties and without the support of the indigenous movement. Correa called a new constitutional assembly in 2007, in which an entirely different balance of forces – Correa's newly-created party was dominant – produced a new and different constitution.

Historically, political volatility has been high in Latin America. In much of the region, military coups and other irregular seizures of power have brought frequent, sudden, and often dramatic reshufflings of rule-writing coalitions. The Mexican presidency changed hands a stunning thirty-six times between 1835 and 1863. Bolivia and Paraguay each experienced more than a dozen coups in the twentieth century alone. Although the post-1978 Third Wave brought an unprecedented level of democratic stability to the region, electoral volatility remains extraordinarily high (Roberts 2014; Mainwaring 2018),[37] and a striking number of elected presidents have been unable to finish their term in office: *twenty-five* Latin American presidents were either impeached or forced to resign amidst protest and impeachment threats between 1978 and 2018 (Pérez-Liñán and Polga-Hecimovich 2018). There is good reason to think that persistent political volatility contributes to institutional instability. Short-term gains in electoral power result in the definition of new rules seeking to strengthen incumbent coalitions, which are then subject to replacement when challengers prevail.[38]

---

[37] There is also evidence that this electoral volatility is rooted in unstable economic conditions. See Roberts and Wibbels (1999); Roberts (2014); Campello and Zucco (2016); and Murillo and Visconti (2017).

[38] Not all coalitions are unstable in Latin America. For example, Albertus and Menaldo's (2018) analysis of authoritarian holdover constitutions highlights the role of coalitional stability. One of the factors that sustain authoritarian constitutions, they argue, is the survival of old guard authoritarian elites and their economic allies. For authoritarian constitutions to break down, they find, the old guard elite must be "dead and gone."

4.3.3 Instability Traps

Institutional instability may also be self-reinforcing. There is reason to think that repeated instances of institutional replacement may generate feedback effects that help to keep the cost of change (C) low. Institutions usually need time to take root. Their persistence over time – through crises and changes in government – often generates greater legitimacy and even "taken-for-grantedness." Thus, a new institution's "susceptibility to pressures for change is greatest early in its life and declines with time" (Henisz and Zelner 2005: 367). Older institutions are also more likely to be embedded in a complex set of layered institutions, formal and informal, and to generate elaborate networks of interconnected actors. This interconnectedness generates a mutually reinforcing effect: when removing one institution affects the functioning of other ones, the number of affected actors increases, thereby expanding the size of coalitions with a stake in preserving the institutional status quo (Pierson 1994, 2000; Hall 2016). Institutional stability also creates incentives for actors to invest in assets and strategies specific to that institution, including, in some cases, coproduction efforts. Such investments strengthen the coalition behind the institution, as actors who develop a stake in particular institutions are more likely to defend them (Pierson 2000).

Where institutions are replaced frequently, by contrast, no such self-reinforcing dynamic emerges. Newly created institutions lack the time to develop widespread public legitimacy and interdependencies with other layered institutions. Moreover, when institutions change repeatedly, actors develop expectations of instability. Because they do not expect new institutions to endure, they are less likely to invest in assets and strategies specific to that institution or engage in coproduction efforts. And because actors do not develop a stake in the institution, or even in institutional stability per se, the coalition in favor of the status quo tends to be weaker, thereby reducing the cost of change (Hall 2016). By contrast, institutional instability generates incentives to invest in extrainstitutional skills and technologies to cope with uncertainty. Those resources, in turn, reduce the cost of institutional replacement and further weaken incentives to keep the institution alive given comparative advantages generated by extrainstitutional investment. Finally, unstable institutions may generate feedback effects by undermining economic and government performance, which creates further pressure for institutional change (Spiller and Tommasi 2007; O'Donnell 1994, 1999). Early rounds of institutional change may thus give rise to what Helmke (2017, forthcoming) calls an "instability trap" – a vicious cycle in which early rounds of institutional change lower the cost of replacement in future rounds.[39]

---

[39] For a related discussion in the context of high courts, see Kapiszewski (2012).

Elkins (2017) and Helmke (2017, forthcoming) offer examples of how the low cost of institutional change may be self-reinforcing. Elkins offers some evidence that constitutions strengthen with age, as citizens come to know, understand, and value them. Older constitutions such as those of Mexico and the United States tend to possess greater legitimacy, which increases the cost of assaulting or replacing them. Thus, repeated constitutional replacement, as we see in countries like Bolivia and Ecuador, may trigger a "negative feedback loop" in which constitutions are never able to develop the legitimacy and citizen attachments required to withstand executive assaults. Likewise, Helmke (2017: 155–160) suggests that polities may fall into an "instability trap," in which repeated constitutional crises erode public trust in (and support for) existing institutional arrangements, which in turn lowers the cost of their replacement in the future.

There is good reason to think, therefore, that institutional instability begets institutional instability. For a particular institutional arrangement to take root, actors must adjust their expectations and behavior to the new rules and procedures. Such adjustments require time (Pierson 2004; Grzymala-Busse 2011). Given a sufficient period of time, actors will invest in strategies appropriate to existing institutional arrangements, and those who succeed under those arrangements will develop both a stake in defending them and the capacity to do so. Early rounds of institutional failure and replacement, however, foreclose such a path. Actors fail to develop stable expectations or strategies appropriate to the existing rules and are thus less likely to develop a stake in their defense. Indeed, as they may come to expect instability, their fear of uncertainty and status quo bias declines. As a result, the cost of institutional replacement remains low.

4.3.4 Compliance and Stability

Compliance and stability are often viewed as complementary. This makes intuitive sense. As the previous section suggests, rules that are widely violated often lack public legitimacy, which leaves them vulnerable to contestation and eventual change (see Helmke 2017: 155–160). In their important study of constitutional stability, Elkins et al. find that "fealty to the dictates of the constitution ... and [constitutional] endurance are inextricably linked" (2009: 77). This is not always the case, however. Indeed, institutional stability is sometimes rooted in the *absence* of such fealty. Noncompliance lowers the stakes surrounding institutional outcomes, which can dampen opposition to those institutions. By shielding potential losers from an institution's effects, forbearance may enhance institutional stability by convincing powerful actors to accept rules that they would otherwise push to overturn. In effect, low compliance can inhibit the emergence of reform coalitions.

The relationship between low compliance and stability can be seen in the case of labor regulations in Latin America. During the 1990s, Latin American governments faced strong pressure to flexibilize their labor markets as a means of attracting investment. Although a few governments (e.g., Peru) dismantled existing labor laws (Murillo 2005), others, such as that of Mexico, opted to maintain the labor code intact while achieving de facto flexibility by instructing bureaucrats to reduce enforcement of labor regulations (Bensusan 2000; Cook 2010). Thus, a labor code established in the 1930s survived the pressures of the Washington Consensus because enforcement agencies could modify its application, permitting lower compliance. Similarly, Argentina's collective labor law – which enables industry-level collective bargaining – remained untouched in the 1990s, largely because the Labor Ministry's decision not to call for industry-wide collective bargaining and instead to push for company-level agreements reduced private-sector pressure for reform (Murillo 2005). When economic and political conditions changed during the 2000s, so too did enforcement, and the number of industry-level agreements increased (Etchemendy and Collier 2007; Etchemendy and Garay 2011).

The stability of weakly enforced institutions is often enhanced by the existence of parallel informal institutions that reduce uncertainty and stabilize actors' behavioral expectations (Helmke and Levitsky 2004). For instance, Mexico's 1917 Constitution was both remarkably stable and weakly enforced. Throughout most of the twentieth century, clauses that threatened the vital interests of the ruling Institutional Revolutionary Party (PRI) and its allies – including free elections, limits of executive power, judicial tenure security, and a variety of social rights – were routinely violated. This arrangement persisted, in part, because an array of informal institutions helped to stabilize politicians' expectations and guide their behavior. For example, the uncertainty generated by presidential succession in a context of noncompetitive elections and a ban on reelection (a rule that was, in fact, strictly enforced) gave rise to an elaborate informal institution, called the *dedazo*, in which presidents unilaterally chose their successor from a select pool of candidates (cabinet members) who followed a set of clear rules (e.g., abstain from publicly seeking or campaigning for the nomination). Outgoing presidents would then retire from political life (Langston 2006). The *dedazo* structured leadership succession for half a century, contributing in an important way to the stability of a constitutional system that was formally democratic but rarely complied with.

Conversely, rules that are regularly enforced and fully complied with may be more vulnerable to instability. In democracies, for example, various aspects of the electoral system (e.g., timing of elections, district magnitude, electoral formulae) are, due to a combination of high visibility and technical necessity, almost always complied with. Losers, therefore, cannot be easily shielded from their effects, which means that they are likely to seek institutional change whenever they have the opportunity. Changes in political power distributions are thus likely to generate pressure for electoral reform. And because political power distributions changed frequently in much of Third Wave Latin America, electoral institutional instability was quite high (Calvo and Negretto forthcoming).

Finally, the activation of previously dormant institutions may permit substantive change – an increase in S – without actually changing the rules. Mexico's democratization, for example, was achieved through greater compliance with the 1917 Constitution rather than its overhaul. Activation may also be seen in the enforcement of social rights in parts of Latin America. Although a wide range of social rights – for example, to health care, housing, and a clean environment – were incorporated into new constitutions across much of Latin America during the 1980s and 1990s, these rights were, for the most part, aspirational; few expected them to be enforced (Klug 2000; Htun 2003: 126). Yet in a few cases, including Brazil and Colombia, civil society organizations mobilized effectively for enforcement, using the legal system to activate constitutional social rights. On several occasions, constitutional court rulings compelled governments to adopt policies aimed at securing these rights (Cepeda-Espinosa 2004; Gauri and Brinks 2008; Brinks and Botero 2014).

Since activation increases S, it may generate new pressure for change from losers who were once shielded from its cost by forbearance, thereby undermining institutional stability. Arguably, recent moves in Brazil to amend the constitution to limit social guarantees are one example of instability prompted by the unexpected strength of the existing institution. An attempt in Colombia in 2011 to force the Constitutional Court to take into account the fiscal impact of its rulings on social and economic rights was quite explicitly a reaction to a court that made social and economic rights a centerpiece of its jurisprudence (Sandoval Rojas and Brinks forthcoming).

5 The Persistence of Institutional Weakness in Latin America

The Third Wave of democratization marked a dramatic change in Latin America. Nearly every country in the region held competitive elections after 1990, and many can now boast at least moderately well-functioning democracies, with clean elections, pluralization of power, effective civil and political rights, increasing citizen participation, and reasonably responsive governments.

There are good reasons to expect three decades of democracy to strengthen political institutions. For one, it is now more difficult for rulers to change laws and constitutions unilaterally. Pluralization of power and, in many countries, political fragmentation means that institutional reform now requires concessions to multiple veto players in exchange for the desired outcome (see, e.g., Brinks and Blass 2018, chapter 6). This should increase the cost of institutional change relative to earlier decades, particularly in democracies with more effective checks and balances.

Democracy has also contributed to the strengthening of enforcement institutions, such as courts and prosecutors (see, e.g., Brinks and Blass 2017, 2018; Couso, Huneeus, and Sieder 2010), as well as the emergence and strengthening of new mechanisms of horizontal accountability (see, e.g., O'Donnell 1998; Mainwaring and Welna 2003). A robust legislative opposition is often crucial to the creation and operation of effective electoral oversight mechanisms (Schedler, Diamond and Plattner 1999). From central banks (Keefer and Stasavage 2003) to judiciaries (Ginsburg 2003; Bill Chavez 2004; Helmke and Ríos Figueroa 2011), greater pluralism should enhance horizontal accountability. The increased autonomy of enforcement regimes from those who wield power should result in greater compliance.

In the shorthand we have employed here, stable democracy and the pluralization of politics should make institutional change more difficult, increasing C, and should also strengthen enforcement mechanisms, increasing V. We would therefore expect, *ceteris paribus*, higher levels of institutional stability, greater compliance, and the activation of previously dormant institutions – in other words, stronger institutions across the board. Political institutions have indeed strengthened in much of Latin America over the last three decades. In many countries, courts are stronger (Couso, Huneeus, and Sieder 2010; Sieder, Schjolden and Angell 2005), electoral laws are better enforced (Mozaffar and Schedler 2002), more social policies are implemented in accordance with universalistic rules (De la O 2015; Garay 2016), some bureaucracies are stronger (Dargent 2015), and in a few cases, enforcement of labor and environmental regulation has improved dramatically (Hochstetler and Keck 2007; Schrank 2011; Amengual 2016). These are, to be sure, significant changes.

Overall, however, institutional strengthening has been modest – and uneven – in Third Wave Latin America. Indeed, problems of institutional instability and low compliance persist throughout much of Latin America. Many of the region's institutions either fail to make a significant difference on the ground or continue to be replaced with striking frequency. What explains this outcome?

In this section, we examine why institutional weakness has persisted in Latin America despite the seemingly favorable conditions generated by the Third Wave of democratization.

5.1 A Problem of Institutional Borrowing?

One possible explanation for the persistence of institutional weakness in Latin America despite democratization could be that the region is prone to naïve institutional borrowing. It may be that cognitive shortcuts and irrational assumptions may have led the region's elites to adopt institutions that do not "fit" the local context since independence (see Weyland 2009). Indeed, Latin American states have long been institutional borrowers in the sense that governments routinely adopt institutional designs whose origins lie outside the country. After independence, for example, postcolonial elites across Latin America borrowed presidentialist constitutions from the United States and legal codes from Western Europe. The pattern of institutional borrowing continued into the Third Wave of democratization. Some imports were actively promoted by international financial institutions; others by transnational advocacy networks. Institutional borrowing was particularly widespread in the 1990s, as many American governments sought to gain international legitimacy vis-à-vis foreign creditors and international financial institutions as they emerged from a decade-long recession provoked by the 1982 Debt Crisis (Murillo 2009). The design of economic, social, legal, electoral, and other reforms was thus heavily influenced by processes of international diffusion (Weyland 2006, 2009).

Scholars debate whether imported institutions are more likely to be weak than are endogenous ones (see, e.g., Weyland 2009; Berkowitz, Pistor, and Richard 2003; Rodrik 2000). It may be, for example, that imported institutions are adopted by narrow technocratic elites or other norm entrepreneurs who are heavily exposed to international norms but have fewer political allies on the ground in their home country. If this is the case, and if the disjuncture between the rule writers and actual power holders is sufficiently large, then the coalition behind imported institutions is likely to be weak. Moreover, institutions that are designed abroad, without regard to the local context, may be more likely to disregard local realities and confront competing social norms, which can limit compliance and reduce incentives for societal coproduction of enforcement. There is, therefore, at least some reason to expect imported institutions to be marked by lower levels of stability and compliance.

Yet there are reasons to question the assumption that imported institutions are necessarily condemned to weakness. Andrew Schrank (forthcoming) shows that imported institutions can gain strength even in a relatively short span of time. As in the case of the civil service scheme for labor inspectors in the

Dominican Republic, imported institutions do, under some conditions, develop roots – and teeth. In Schrank's case study, these conditions include strong (often external) incentives for governments to invest in enforcing borrowed institutions, a sustained effort by state officials to build a coalition of support for the new institution, and crucially, partners in society who work to generate compliance in the face of often divergent societal norms. Hence, imported institutions have clear obstacles to overcome if they are to become stable and effective. Yet, these obstacles are not different in kind from the ones many homegrown institutions must overcome (Schrank forthcoming). Whether institutions are designed at home or borrowed from abroad, rule makers must forge domestic coalitions to ensure their enforcement and stability.

5.2 Mechanisms that Reproduce Institutional Weakness in Latin America

What, then, explains the persistence of weak institutions, even after three decades of democracy, in much of Latin America? We suggest that three interconnected factors, which reflect some of the perennial economic and political realities of the region, play an important role in reproducing its institutional weakness. The first is socioeconomic inequality. Extreme inequality reinforces institutional weakness in several ways. For one, under democracy, it generates social and political pressure for governments to adopt ambitious institutional reforms that are difficult to enforce. Thus, unequal democracies are more likely to give rise to window dressing institutions, aspirational rights, and ambitious laws and regulations that fail to elicit widespread compliance. In such a context, the wealthy can more easily buy off state officials, converting them into their agents. Aspirational laws also elicit uneven compliance in a context of extreme inequality. As Htun and Jensenius (forthcoming) show in their analysis of violence against women legislation in Mexico, women with education, secure employment, and considerable financial resources are more likely to comply with the law and thus gain its benefits. In general, then, the higher the level of socioeconomic (or ethnic, regional, gender, or other) inequality, the more likely it is that institutions will be unevenly enforced or complied with (see Lieberman 2003).

As Holland's work on forbearance (2017, forthcoming) makes clear, uneven compliance does not always favor the rich. Inequality reduces the likelihood that the poor will exert influence in the national-level arenas where laws are designed. However, the all-too-visible cost of actually enforcing laws that impose great harm on poor people – like laws prohibiting squatting and street vending – generates powerful pressure for local governments to engage in forbearance. In this case, then, selective enforcement favors the poor in the short term while reducing incentives for redistribution through public policy in the longer term.

Another factor reinforcing institutional weakness is the persistence of weak state capacity (Centeno 2002; O'Donnell 1993). In terms of fiscal capacity, Latin American states remain considerably weaker than their counterparts in Europe and East Asia (Cardenas 2010). Early patterns of state weakness, rooted in factors such as social inequality, the nature of interstate conflict, and the timing of the region's insertion into the global economy, persisted over time.[40] Limited capacity thus helps explain the standoffish nature of many Latin American states, as well as the incentives for governments to use forbearance as an informal social policy instead of investing in formal welfare states. Weak states with limited revenues must pick and choose their enforcement battles.

Institutional weakness has been reinforced by persistent economic and political volatility. Economic shocks such as high inflation, recession, and commodity boom-and-bust cycles remain a common occurrence in most of Latin America. As a producer of natural resources dependent on external capital, the region has long been vulnerable to boom and bust cycles (Campello and Zucco 2016). Economic shocks disrupt distributive coalitions and generate higher levels of public discontent, which contribute to higher levels of institutional instability. Economic shocks have hardly diminished during the democratic era. Indeed, in the last 35 years alone, Latin America has experienced the debt crisis and soaring inflation of the 1980s, the "lost half-decade" of 1998–2002, and the extraordinary commodities boom-and-bust cycle of 2002–2014 (Bértola and Ocampo 2012). As a result, pressure for policy and institutional change remains strikingly high.

Political volatility also remains high. Contrary to widespread expectations, few Latin American party systems stabilized over the course of the Third Wave. Levels of electoral volatility, which were among the highest in the world in the 1990s, remained strikingly high (Roberts 2014; Mainwaring 2018). Indeed, many of the region's party systems (e.g., Argentina, Colombia, Costa Rica, Guatemala, Honduras, Mexico, Peru, Venezuela) grew considerably *more* fragmented and volatile during the early twenty-first century. Although healthy political pluralism may contribute to institutional strength, extreme fragmentation and electoral volatility can be an important source of institutional instability. As long as Latin American democracies are characterized by frequent and

---

[40] On the origins of state weakness in the region, see Centeno (2002); Coatsworth (2008); Mahoney (2010); Kurtz (2013); Soifer (2015).

far-reaching shifts in governing coalitions and therefore rule makers, many political institutions are likely to remain unstable.

These observations suggest that the persistence of institutional weakness in Latin America is rooted in economic and political conditions that have long afflicted the region: state weakness, high socioeconomic inequality, and economic and political volatility. Worse, there is reason to think that these conditions are, at least in part, a function of institutional weaknesses. Thus, much of Latin America may be suffering from a self-reinforcing cycle in which inequality and economic and political volatility produce institutional weakness, which, in turn, generates additional inequality and instability. Given the widespread adoption of ambitious institutions since democratization, these conditions are likely to erode part of the gains promised by expanded rights resulting from civil society mobilization and political incorporation.

5.3 Democracy and Institutional Ambition

Finally, democracy itself, paradoxically, may reinforce institutional weakness in Latin America by generating pressure for the design of more ambitious institutions. Democratization permitted the emergence of a revitalized civil society. Free to organize without fear of repression, a diversity of civic groups mobilized in pursuit of ambitious socioeconomic and political goals during the late twentieth and early twenty-first centuries. Whether it was indigenous groups in Bolivia and Ecuador, landless and environmental movements in Brazil, unemployed workers in Argentina, or students in Chile, social movements across Latin America pushed governments to adopt new rights, protections, and other inclusionary reforms (Silva and Rossi 2018). At the same time, electoral competition – in a context of extreme social inequality – generated incentives for politicians to embrace and advance these reforms. Indeed, Latin America's electoral turn to the Left in the early twenty-first century gave rise to a range of new institutions and policies aimed at appealing to previously marginalized constituencies (Levitsky and Roberts 2011). Examples include the inclusion of diverse social rights (Gauri and Brinks 2008; Elkins et al. 2009) and indigenous rights (Yashar 2005) in new constitutions, the creation of new participatory institutions (Wampler 2009; Mayka 2018) and mechanisms of prior consultation (Falleti and Riofrancos 2018), the unprecedented creation of universalistic social policies (Garay 2016), and the adoption of gender and racial quota laws (Htun 2015), antidomestic violence laws (Htun and Jensenius forthcoming), and laws protecting the rights of domestic workers.

These new institutions were designed to pursue far-reaching goals. In other words, they were highly ambitious – io' in Figure 1. Compliance with these new institutions varied. But even where governments invested heavily in enforcement, thereby increasing io and S in Figure 1, the gap between institutional ambition (io′) and actual compliance (io) was vast. Thus, democracy has given rise to highly ambitious institutions that, in many instances, have brought real behavioral change. But at the same time, gaps between ambition and outcomes have persisted and even grown. Such insufficient compliance reinforces perceptions of institutional weakness.

6 Conclusion

We began this Element with the premise that what ultimately distinguishes strong institutions from weak ones is that the former matter more than the latter. The same institution, in two different contexts or at two different times, is stronger if it makes more of a behavioral difference in one instance than in the other. However, it can be difficult to evaluate exactly how much an institution "matters." It is relatively simple to establish that an institution is strong because, on paper, it possesses features that should make it matter – for example, it commands great things. But it is an altogether different – and, we believe, far more interesting – thing to say that an institution is strong because it actually produces an outcome that is substantially different from what we might have observed in its absence, and that it continues to produce that outcome even in the face of pressures to change it or avoid it altogether.

In this Element, we have offered an initial framework for studying institutional weakness. We conceptualize institutional strength based on the actual and expected effects of the institution. That is, our measure of institutional strength depends conceptually on the distance between the mandated behavior and the actual behavior. Even though measurement strategies will sometimes diverge from that, we should keep in mind that the goal ultimately is to uncover the difference between what the world would look like in the absence of the institution and what it looks like with the institution. This conceptualization allows us to classify institutional weakness into three types: insignificance, noncompliance, and instability.

Distinguishing among types of institutional weakness allowed us to develop some initial hypotheses about the conditions underlying the variation in institutional strength that we observe in Latin America. First, international donors and transnational activist coalitions lead to high returns to institutional innovation per se, with little regard for real world effects. This leads to the adoption of formally ambitious but weakly enforced institutions. Institutions that seek to change dominant social norms and informal institutions face especially high challenges. Changing social norms and the increasing autonomy of enforcement mechanisms in Latin America over the last three or four decades, however, began to separate the politics of compliance from the politics of design, leading, at least in some cases, to activation. In future rounds of institutional creation, this may place a greater premium on the politics of design, as opponents cannot count on simply ignoring the institution. Instead, opponents will have to negotiate for less ambitious institutions, or loopholes and weaknesses in the formal design itself, seeking to make the institution insignificant. On the other hand, a disjuncture between designers and enforcers can lead to low compliance when enforcers do not share the institution's goals. Noncompliance and instability generate negative feedback, as institutions fail to develop strong constituencies of support. This often results in greater instability, as it allows political competition and recurring crises to produce cycling preferences in the ruling coalition, with a constant politics of repeal and replace and few actors lobbying for institutional preservation. Institutional imports are simply a special case of this last point: they fail when they do not put down roots, but can succeed when they develop a supportive coalition.

Our goal here was to clarify some of the conceptual and theoretical underpinnings of work on institutions that fail to produce the outcomes they were ostensibly designed to produce. Research on institutional weakness is reshaping our understanding of how politics works in Latin America and elsewhere. It has taught us, for example, that when actors design or reform institutions, they consider not only the rules' substance but also the likelihood of their compliance and endurance. Some institutions (e.g., window dressing laws) are created precisely because actors do not expect compliance. Others (e.g., aspirational laws) are created not in the knowledge that they will be complied with in the short term, but in the hope that they will reshape norms and behavior in the longer term. Alternatively, actors may create rules that they expect to comply with in the short term but not in the long term (e.g., presidential term limits in twenty-first century Bolivia and Venezuela). This variation in expected compliance and stability affects political behavior, strategies, and outcomes in important ways. Indeed, research that takes this variation seriously has led scholars to rethink and revise important institutionalist theories in comparative and Latin American politics.

Future research could further this agenda by exploring which types of institution are most (and least) vulnerable to particular kinds of weakness. Due to differences in the cost and feasibility of monitoring, for example, some institutions are undoubtedly easier to enforce than others. Likewise, some institutions are easier to change – and perhaps more prone to "instability traps" – than others. Building generalizable theories about these differences would be an important contribution to comparative research.

Another area for future work lies in measurement. We need better indicators of institutional weakness. How, for example, do we determine whether a legal change signals a pattern of instability as opposed to being an instance of adaptation? How do we compare institutional strength when levels of ambition vary? Which is stronger: a highly ambitious institution that is only partially complied with or a low-ambition institution that is completely or mostly complied with? Compliance may be higher in the latter case, but the former may nevertheless generate greater movement away from the preinstitutional outcome.

Measuring institutional weakness is difficult. For example, because noncompliance entails rule-breaking, actors often seek to hide or disguise it, which often results in problems of underreporting and undercounting. Scholars seeking to measure low compliance may rely on observed violations, frequency of sanctions, examination of the resources invested into enforcement, or societal coproduction of enforcement efforts. Insignificance poses a different problem: because everyone complies with the rule, insignificant institutions may be easily confused with strong ones. Assessing insignificance may thus require counterfactual analysis of the state of the world in the absence of the relevant institution. Instability is easier to observe but harder to interpret because it may easily be confused with adaptation. Distinguishing instability from adaptation may entail either theorizing a "regular" rate of change or employing average rates – within the region or over time – as a comparative benchmark. Good indicators and measurement strategies are critical to scholars' ability to engage in comparative analysis of institutional weakness and its effects across cases.

To conclude, it is worth emphasizing that institutional weakness helps to broaden our understanding of how power distributions shape rule makers' choices in a context of high socioeconomic inequality – a phenomenon that is emerging in advanced economies as well. Extreme power inequalities, embedded in a context of formally democratic regimes and a liberal international environment, powerfully shape actors' choices in the design and enforcement of formal institutions. In such a context, we see some rules that are designed not to be enforced; rules that are designed to be complied with by some but not by others; and rules that are politically appealing to the designers but are vetoed, on the ground, by those charged with enforcement. We see standoffish states that enforce rules intermittently or selectively, depending on the coalition in power or the degree to which societal actors mobilize to support or oppose them.

Earlier work has already shown how power differentials shape the political coalitions defining how institutions are designed, as well as their subsequent effects (Hall 2016; Knight 1992; Moe 2005; Pierson 2016). By theorizing the politics of institutional weakness, our analysis provides a more complete view of the strategies political actors may employ at all stages of an institution's life cycle, but especially during creation. Expectations regarding the degree and type of weakness likely affect the politics of institutional creation and change. Weakness is often designed into institutions; in other instances actors agree to nominally strong institutions with the expectation of noncompliance. Explicit attention to the causes of instability is likely to enrich theories about the time horizons and expectations of institutional designers. Theorizing the roots of noncompliance can help us understand when powerful actors agree to institutional changes that seem obviously adverse to their interests; or when institutions persist over time even though they appear to challenge deep power structures or social norms.

The claim that "institutions matter" has long been met with the retort that, in Latin America, weakness renders formal institutions irrelevant at best, and misleading at worst. The framework we present here is a step toward understanding not only when institutions do or do not matter, but also how institutional weakness may be deployed as a strategy in power struggles involving both strong and weak actors.

References

Aisen, Ari and Francisco Veiga. 2013. "How Does Political Instability Affect Economic Growth?" *European Journal of Political Economy* 29: 151–167.

Albertus, Michael and Victor Menaldo. 2018. *Authoritarianism and the Elite Origins of Democracy.* New York: Cambridge University Press.

Forthcoming. "The Stickiness of 'Bad' Institutions: Constitutional Continuity and Change Under Democracy." In Daniel M. Brinks, Steven Levitsky and M. Victoria Murillo, (eds.), *Understanding Institutional Weakness: Lessons from Latin America* New York: Cambridge University Press.

Amengual, Matthew. 2014. "Pathways to Enforcement: Labor Inspectors Leveraging Linkages with Society in Argentina." *ILR Review* 67(1): 3–33.

2016. *Politicized Enforcement in Argentina: Labor and Environmental Regulation.* New York: Cambridge University Press.

Amengual, Matthew and Eduardo Dargent. Forthcoming. "The Social Determinants of Enforcement: Integrating Politics with Limited State Capacity." In Daniel M. Brinks, Steven Levitsky and M. Victoria Murillo, eds., *Understanding Institutional Weakness: Lessons from Latin America.* New York: Cambridge University Press.

Anria, Santiago. 2013. "Social Movements, Party Organization and Populism: Insights from the Bolivian MAS," *Latin American Politics and Society* 55 (3): 19–46.

Bensusán, Graciela. 2000. *El Modelo Mexicano de Regulación Laboral.* Xochimilco: Plaza y Valdés.

Berggren, Niclas, Andreas Bergh, and Christian Bjørnskor. 2011. "The Growth Effects of Institutional Instability." *Journal of Institutional Economics* 8 (2): 187–224.

Bergman, Marcelo. 2009. *Tax Evasion and the Rule of Law in Latin America.* University Park: Pennsylvania State University Press.

Berkowitz, Daniel, Katharina Pistor, and Jean-Francois Richard. 2003. "The Transplant Effect." *American Journal of Comparative Law* 51(1): 163–203.

Bértola, Luis and José Antonio Ocampo. 2012. *The Economic Development of Latin America since Independence.* Oxford: Oxford University Press.

Bill Chavez, Rebecca. 2004. *The Rule of Law in Nascent Democracies: Judicial Politics in Argentina.* Redwood City: Stanford University Press.

Boix, Carles. 1999. "Setting the Rules of the Game: The Choice of Electoral Systems in Advanced Democracies." *American Political Science Review* 93(3): 609–24.

Brinks, Daniel M. 2003. "Informal Institutions and the Rule of Law: The Judicial Response to State Killings in Buenos Aires and São Paulo in the 1990s." *Comparative Politics* 36 (1): 1–19.

2019. "Access to What? Legal Agency and Access to Justice for Indigenous Peoples in Latin America." *Journal of Development Studies* 55 (3): 348–365.

Brinks, Daniel M. and Abby Blass. 2013. "Beyond the Façade: Institutional Engineering and Potemkin Courts in Latin America, 1975–2009." Unpublished. Available at www.academia.edu/15429591/Beyond_the_Fac_ade_Institutional_Engineering_and_Potemkin_Courts_in_Latin_America_1975–2009.

2017. "Rethinking Judicial Empowerment: The New Foundations of Constitutional Justice." *International Journal of Constitutional Law* 15(2): 296–331.

2018. *The DNA of Constitutional Justice in Latin America: Politics, Governance, and Judicial Design*. Cambridge: Cambridge University Press.

Brinks, Daniel M. and Sandra Botero. 2014. "Inequality and the Rule of Law: Ineffective Rights in Latin American Democracies." In *Reflections on Uneven Democracies: The Legacy of Guillermo O'Donnell*, Daniel M. Brinks, Marcelo Leiras and Scott Mainwaring, eds. Baltimore: Johns Hopkins University Press.

Büthe, Tim and Helen Milner. 2008. "The Politics of Foreign Direct Investment into Developing Countries: Increasing FDI Through Trade Agreements?" *American Journal of Political Science* 52 (4): 741–762.

Calvo, Ernesto and Gabriel Negretto. Forthcoming. "When (Electoral) Opportunity Knocks: Weak Institutions, Political Shocks, and Electoral Reforms in Latin America." In Daniel M. Brinks, Steven Levitsky and M. Victoria Murillo, eds., *Understanding Institutional Weakness: Lessons from Latin America*. New York: Cambridge University Press.

Calvo, Ernesto and Juan Pablo Micozzi. 2005. "The Governor's Backyard: A Seat-Vote Model of Electoral Reform for Subnational Multiparty Races." The Journal of Politics 67, no. 4 (November 2005): 1050–1074.

Campello, Daniela and Cesar Zucco Jr. 2016. "Presidential Success and the World Economy." *Journal of Politics* 78 (2): 589–602.

Cardenas, Mauricio. 2010. "State Capacity in Latin America." *Economia* 10 (2): 1–45.

Carey, John. 1996. *Term Limits and Legislative Representation*. Cambridge: Cambridge University Press.

Carpenter, Daniel P. 2001. *The Forging of Bureaucratic Autonomy: Reputations, Networks, and Policy Innovation in Executive Agencies, 1862–1928*. Princeton: Princeton University Press.

Carrubba, Cliff. 2009. "A Model of the Endogenous Development of Judicial Institutions in Federal and International Systems." *Journal of Politics* 71 (1): 55–69.

Centeno, Miguel Angel. 2002. *Of Blood and Debt: War and the Nation-State in Latin America*. University Park: Penn State University Press.

Center for Reproductive Rights. 2014. *A Pivotal Moment: 2014 Annual Report*. New York: Center for Reproductive Rights. Available at www .reproductiverights.org/sites/crr.civicactions.net/files/documents/CRR-192014-Annual-Report.pdf.

Cepeda Espinosa, Manuel J. (2004). "Judicial Activism in a Violent Context: The Origin, Role and Impact of the Colombian Constitutional Court." *Washington University Global Studies Law Review* 3: 529.

Coatsworth, John. 2008. "Inequality, Institutions, and Economic Growth in Latin America," *Journal of Latin American Studies* 40: 545–569.

Conran, James, and Kathleen A. Thelen. 2016. "Institutional Change." In *The Oxford Handbook of Historical Institutionalism*. Edited by Orfeo Fioretos, Tulia G. Falleti, and Adam Sheingate. Oxford: Oxford University Press: 51–70.

Corrales, Javier and Michael Penfold. 2014. "Manipulating Term Limits in Latin America." *Journal of Democracy* 25 (4): 157–68.

Coslovsky, Salo V. 2011. "Relational Regulation in the Brazilian Ministerio Publico: The Organizational Basis of Regulatory Responsiveness." *Regulation & Governance* 5: 70–89.

Couso, Javier, Alexandra Huneeus, and Rachel Sieder, eds. 2010. *Cultures of Legality: Judicialization and Political Activism in Latin America*. New York: Cambridge University Press.

Cox, Gary and Matthew McCubbins. 2002. "The Institutional Determinants of Economic Policy Outcomes." In Haggard, S. and McCubbins, M. (eds.), *Presidents, Parliaments and Policy*, New York: Cambridge University Press.

Crawford, Sue E. S. and Elinor Ostrom. 1995. "A Grammar of Institutions." *American Political Science Review* 89: 582–600.

Crawford, Sue E. S. and Elinor Ostrom. 1995. "A Grammar of Institutions." *American Political Science Review* 89: 582–600.

Crisp, Brian and Juan Carlos Rey. 2003. "The Sources of Electoral Reform in Venezuela." In Matthew Shugart and Martin Wattenberg, eds., *Mixed-Member Electoral Systems: The Best of Both Worlds?* Oxford: Oxford University Press.

Dargent, Eduardo. 2015. Technocracy and Democracy in Latin America. New York: Cambridge University Press.

Dargent, Eduardo, Andreas E. Feldmann, and Juan Pablo Luna. 2017. "Greater State Capacity, Lesser Stateness: Lessons from the Peruvian Commodity Boom." *Politics and Society* 45(1): 3–34.

De la Torre, Carlos. 2010. *Populist Seduction in Latin America*. Ohio State University Press.

Dobbin, Frank, Beth Simmons, and Geoffrey Garrett. 2007. "The Global Diffusion of Public Policies: Social Construction, Coercion, Competition, or Learning?" *Annual Review of Sociology* 33: 449–72.

Eisenstadt, Todd, Daniela Stevens Leon, and Marcela Torres Wong. 2017. "Does Prior Consultation Diminish Extractive Conflict or Just Channel It to New Venues? Evidence from a Survey and Cases in Latin America." Paper presented at the 2017 Meeting of the Latin American Studies Association, May 1, 2017. Lima, Peru.

Elkins, Zachary 2017. "A Militant Defense of Term Limits in Bolivia." Paper presented at the Conference on Weak Institutions, at the University of Texas at Austin, September 28, 2017. *Understanding Institutional Weakness: Lessons from Latin America*, unpublished manuscript.

Elkins, Zachary, Tom Ginsburg, and James Melton. 2009. *The Endurance of National Constitutions*. Cambridge: Cambridge University Press.

Elkins, Zachary, Andrew Guzman and Beth Simmons. 2006. "Competing for Capital: the Diffusion of Bilateral Investment Treaties, 1960–2000." *International Organization* 60 (Fall): 811–846.

Ellickson, Robert C. 1991. *Order Without Law*. Cambridge: Harvard University Press.

Epstein, Lee, Jack Knight and Olga Shvetsova. (2001). "The Role of Constitutional Courts in the Establishment and Maintenance of Democratic Systems of Government." *Law & Society Review* 35(1): 117–164.

Etchemendy, Sebastian and Ruth Collier. 2007. "Down but Not Out: Union Resurgence and Segmented Neocorporatism in Argentina (2003–2007)," *Politics and Society* 35 (3): 363–401.

Falleti, Tulia, "Social Origins of Institutional Strength: Prior Consultation over Extraction of Hydrocarbons in Bolivia." In Daniel M. Brinks, Steven Levitsky and M. Victoria Murillo, eds., *Understanding Institutional Weakness: Lessons from Latin America*. New York: Cambridge University Press.

Falleti, Tulia and Thea Riofrancos. 2018. "Endogenous Participation: Strengthening Prior Consultation in Extractive Economies." *World Politics* 70 (1): 86–121.

Fernández Milmanda, Belen and Candelaria Garay. 2008. "A Multilevel Approach to Enforcement: Forest Protection in the Argentine Chaco."

In Daniel M. Brinks, Steven Levitsky and M. Victoria Murillo, eds., *Understanding Institutional Weakness: Lessons from Latin America.* New York: Cambridge University Press

Ferraz, Octavio L. M. 2010. "Harming the Poor Through Social Rights Litigation: Lessons from Brazil." Texas Law Review 89: 1643–1668.

Gauri, Varun and Daniel M. Brinks, eds. 2008. *Courting Social Justice: Judicial Enforcement of Social and Economic Rights in the Developing World.* New York: Cambridge University Press.

Gingerich, Daniel W. 2013. "Governance Indicators and the Level of Analysis Problem: Empirical Findings from South America." *British Journal of Political Science* 43(3): 505–40.

Ginsburg, Tom. 2003. *Judicial Independence in New Democracies: Constitutional Courts in Asian Cases.* New York: Cambridge University Press.

Giraudy, Augustina and Juan Pablo Luna. 2017. "Unpacking the State's Uneven Territorial Reach: Evidence from Latin America" in M. Centeno, A. Kohli, and D. Yashar, eds., *States in the Developing World*, New York: Cambridge University Press.

Grzymala-Busse, Anna. 2011. Time Will Tell? Temporality and the Analysis of Causal Mechanisms and Processes. *Comparative Political Studies.* 44/9: 1267–1297.

Gonzalez Ocantos, Ezequiel, Chad Kiewiet de Jonge, and David W. Nickerson. 2014. "The Conditionality of Vote-Buying Norms: Experimental Evidence from Latin America." *American Journal of Political Science* 58(1): 197–211.

Grindle, Merilee. 2012. "Good Governance: The Inflation of an Idea." In *Planning Ideas That Matter: Livability, Territoriality, Governance, and Reflective Practice.* Edited by Bishwapriya Sanyal, Lawrence J. Vale, Christina D. Rosan. Boston: MIT Press: 259–82.

Hacker, Jacob S. 2005. "Policy Drift: The Hidden Politics of US Welfare State Retrenchment." In Wolfgang Streek and Kathleen Thelen, eds., *Beyond Continuity: Institutional Change in Advanced Political Economies.* Oxford: Oxford University Press: 40–82.

Hall, Peter. 2016. "Politics as a Process Structured in Space and Time" in Fioretos, O., Falleti, T., and Sheingate, A. (eds.), *Handbook of Historical Institutionalism*, Oxford: Oxford University Press.

Hart, H. L. A. 1961. *The Concept of Law.* Oxford: Oxford University Press.

Hellman, Judith. 1983. *Mexico in Crisis.* New York: Holmes & Meier Publishers

Helmke, Gretchen. 2004. *Courts under Constraints: Judges, Generals, and Presidents in Argentina.* Cambridge: Cambridge University Press.

2017. *Institutions on the Edge: The Origins and Consequences of Inter-Branch Crises in Latin America.* Cambridge: Cambridge University Press.

2018. "Presidential Crises in Contemporary Latin America." In Daniel M. Brinks, Steven Levitsky and M. Victoria Murillo, eds., *Understanding Institutional Weakness: Lessons from Latin America.* New York: Cambridge University Press.

Helmke, Gretchen and Steven Levitsky. 2004. "Informal Institutions and Comparative Politics: A Research Agenda." *Perspectives on Politics 2* (4): 725–740.

Helmke, Gretchen and Steven Levitsky, eds. 2006. *Informal Institutions and Democracy: Lessons from Latin America.* Baltimore: Johns Hopkins University Press.

Helmke, Gretchen and Julio Ríos-Figueroa, eds. 2011. *Courts in Latin America.* Cambridge: Cambridge University Press.

Henisz, Witold. 2002. *Politics and International Investment: Measuring Risk and Protecting Profits.* Cheltenham, UK: Edward Elgar Publishing.

Henisz, Witold, Bennet A. Zelner, and Mauro F. Guillén. 2005. "The Worldwide Diffusion of Market-Oriented Infrastructure Reform, 1977–1999." *American Sociological Review* 70 (6): 871–897.

Herbst, Jeffrey. 2000. *States and Power in Africa.* Princeton: Princeton University Press.

Hochstetler, Kathryn and Margaret Keck. 2007. *Greening Brazil: Environmental Activism in State and Society.* Durham: Duke University Press.

Holland, Alisha C. 2017. *Forbearance as Redistribution: The Politics of Informal Welfare in Latin America.* Cambridge: Cambridge University Press.

2018. "Coercion Gaps." In Daniel M. Brinks, Steven Levitsky and M. Victoria Murillo, eds., *Understanding Institutional Weakness: Lessons from Latin America.* New York: Cambridge University Press.

Htun, Mala. 2003. *Sex and the State.* Cambridge: Cambridge University Press.

Htun, Mala and Francesca Jensenius. Forthcoming. "Aspirational Laws as Weak Institutions: Legislation to Combat Violence against Women in Mexico." In Daniel M. Brinks, Steven Levitsky and M. Victoria Murillo, eds., *Understanding Institutional Weakness: Lessons from Latin America.* New York: Cambridge University Press.

Huber, Gregory A. 2007. *The Craft of Bureaucratic Neutrality: Interests and Influence in Governmental Regulation of Occupational Safety.* Cambridge: Cambridge University Press.

Huber, John D. and Charles R. Shipan. 2002. *Deliberate Discretion? The Institutional Foundations of Bureaucratic Autonomy.* Cambridge: Cambridge University Press.

Kapiszewski, Diana. 2012. *High Courts and Economic Governance in Argentina and Brazil*. Cambridge: Cambridge University Press.

Keck, Margaret and Kathryn Sikkink. 1998. *Activists Beyond Borders: Transnational Activist Networks in International Politics*. Ithaca: Cornell University Press.

Keefer, Philip and David Stasavage. 2003. "The Limits of Delegation: Veto Players, Central Bank Independence, and the Credibility of Monetary Policy." *American Political Science Review* 97(3): 407–23.

Keyssar, Alexander. 2000. *The Right to Vote: The Contested History of Democracy in the United States*. New York: Basic Books.

Knight, Alan. 1986. *The Mexican Revolution Vol. 1: Porfirians, Liberals and Peasants*. Cambridge: Cambridge University Press.

Knight, Jack. 1992. *Institutions and Social Conflict*. New York: Cambridge University Press.

Krasner, Stephen. 1988. "Sovereignty: An Institutional Perspective." *Comparative Political Studies* 21: 66–94.

Kurtz, Marcus J. 2013. *Latin American State Building in Comparative Perspective: Social Foundations of Institutional Order*. Cambridge: Cambridge University Press.

Landau, David. 2017. "Judicial Role and the Limits of Constitutional Convergence in Latin America," 227–252, in Rosalind Dixon and Tom Ginsburg, eds., *Comparative Constitutional Law in Latin America*. Cheltenham, UK: Edward Elgar Publishing.

Langford, Malcolm, Ben Cousins, Jackie Dugard, and Tshepo Madlingozi, eds. 2011. *Symbols or Substance? The Role and Impact of Socio-Economic Rights Strategies in South Africa*. Cambridge: Cambridge University Press.

Levi, Margaret. 1997. *Consent, Dissent and Patriotism*. Cambridge: Cambridge University Press.

1988. *Of Rule and Revenue*. Berkeley: University of California Press.

Levitsky, Steven and María Victoria Murillo. 2009. "Variation in Institutional Strength." *Annual Review of Political Science* 12: 115–33.

2013. "Building Institutions on Weak Foundations." *Journal of Democracy* 24(2): 93–107.

2014. "Building Institutions on Weak Foundations: Lessons from Latin America." In Daniel Brinks, Marcelo Leiras, and Scott Mainwaring (eds.), *Reflections on Uneven Democracies. The Legacy of Guillermo O'Donnell*, Johns Hopkins University Press.

Levy, Brian and Pablo Spiller (eds.). 1996. *Regulations, Institutions, and Commitment: Comparative Studies of Telecommunications*. New York: Cambridge University Press.

Lieberman, Evan S. 2003. *Race and Regionalism in the Politics of Taxation in Brazil and South Africa*. Cambridge: Cambridge University Press.

Lipsky, Michael. 2010. *Street Level Bureaucracy: Dilemmas of the Individual in Public Service*. New York: Russell Sage Foundation.

Loveman, Brian. 1994. "'Protected Democracies' and Military Guardianship: Political Transitions in Latin America, 1978–1993." *Journal of Interamerican Studies and World Affairs* 36(2): 105–89.

Madrid, Raul. 2012. *The Rise of Ethnic Politics in Latin America*. Cambridge: Cambridge University Press.

Mahoney, James. 2010. *Colonialism and Postcolonial Development: Spanish America in Comparative Perspective*, New York: Cambridge University Press

Mahoney, James and Kathleen Thelen. 2010. "A Theory of Gradual Institutional Change." In *Explaining Institutional Change: Ambiguity, Agency, and Power*. Edited by James Mahoney and Kathleen Thelen. Cambridge: Cambridge University Press: 1–37.

Mainwaring, Scott. 2018. "Party System Institutionalization in Contemporary Latin America." In Scott Mainwaring, ed., *Party Systems in Latin America. Institutionalization, Decay and Collapse*, New York: Cambridge University Press.

Mainwaring, Scott and Christopher Welna, eds. 2003. *Democratic Accountability in Latin America*. Oxford: Oxford University Press.

Mann, Michael. 1984. "The Autonomous Power of the State: Its Origins, Mechanisms and Results." *European Journal of Sociology* 25: 185–213.

Mares, Isabela. 2005. "Social Protection Around the World: External Insecurity, State Capacity, and Domestic Political Cleavages." *Comparative Political Studies*, 38 (6): 623–651.

Méndez, Juan E., Paulo Sérgio Pinheiro, and Guillermo O'Donnell, eds. 1999. *(Un)Rule of Law and the Underprivileged in Latin America*. Notre Dame: Notre Dame University Press.

Migdal, Joel S. 1988. *Strong Societies and Weak States: State-Society Relations and State Capabilities in the Third World*. Princeton: Princeton University Press.

Moe, Terry. 1990. "Political Institutions: The Neglected Side of the Story," *Journal of Law, Economics and Organization*, 6 (special issue): 213–253.
2005. "Power and Political Institutions." *Perspectives on Politics* 3 (2): 215–233.

Moncada, Eduardo. 2016. *Cities, Business, and the Politics of Urban Violence in Latin America*. Stanford: Stanford University Press.

Mozaffar, Shaheen and Andreas Schedler. 2002. "The Comparative Study of Electoral Governance." *International Political Science Review* 23(1): 5–27.

Murillo, Maria Victoria. 2009. *Political Competition, Partisanship, and Policymaking in Latin America*. Cambridge: Cambridge University Press.

Murillo, María Victoria, Lucas Ronconi, and Andrew Schrank. 2011. "Latin American Labor Reforms: Evaluating Risk and Security." José Antonio Ocampo and Jaime Ros, eds., *Oxford Handbook of Latin American Economics*. Oxford: Oxford University Press: 790–812.

Murillo, María Victoria and Giancarlo Visconti. 2017. "Economic Performance and Incumbents' Support in Latin America." *Electoral Studies* 45:180–190.

Murray, Rainbow. 2004. "Why Didn't Parity Work? A Closer Examination of the 2002 Election Results." *French Politics* 2: 347–362.

 2007. "How Parties Evaluate Compulsory Quotas: A Study of the Implementation of the 'Parity' Law in France." *Parliamentary Affairs* 60(4): 568–584.

Nichter, Simeon. 2011. "Vote Buying in Brazil: From Impunity to Prosecution." Unpublished. Available at https://projects.iq.harvard.edu/files/ruling_politics/files/nichter_-_vote_buying_in_brazil_-_from_impunity_to_prosecution.pdf.

North, Douglass C. 1990. *Institutions, Institutional Change and Economic Performance*. Cambridge: Cambridge University Press.

O'Donnell, Guillermo A. 1993. "On the State, Democratization and Some Conceptual Problems: A Latin American View with Glances at Some Postcommunist Countries." *World Development* 21(8): 1355–69.

 1994. "Delegative Democracy." *Journal of Democracy* 5(1): 55–69.

 1998. "Horizontal Accountability in New Democracies." *Journal of Democracy* 9(3): 112–26.

 1999. *Counterpoints: Selected Essays on Authoritarianism and Democratization*. South Bend: University of Notre Dame Press.

 2004. "Why the Rule of Law Matters." *Journal of Democracy* 15(4): 32–46.

Oquendo, Angel. 2006. *Latin American Law*. New York: Foundation Press, Thomson/West.

Ostrom, Elinor. 1986. "An Agenda for the Study of Institutions." *Public Choice* 48(1): 3–25.

 1996. "Crossing the Great Divide: Co-production, Synergy, and Development." *World Development* 24(6): 1073–87.

Palier, Bruno. 2005. "Ambiguous Agreement, Cumulative Change: French Social Policy in the 1990s." In *Beyond Continuity: Institutional Change in Advanced Political Economies*. Edited by Wolfgang Streeck and Kathleen Ann Thelen. Oxford: Oxford University Press, 127–144.

Pérez-Liñán, Aníbal. 2007. *Presidential Impeachment and the New Political Instability in Latin America*. Cambridge: Cambridge University Press.

Pérez-Liñán, Aníbal and John Polga-Hecimovich. 2018. *Executive Exits in the Americas (version 2018-6-26)*. University of Notre Dame.

Peters, B. Guy. 2011. *Institutional Theory in Political Science: The New Institutionalism*. London: Bloomsbury Publishing.

Pierson, Paul. 1994. *Dismantling the Welfare State?: Reagan, Thatcher and the Politics of Retrenchment*. Cambridge: Cambridge University Press.

    2000. "Increasing Returns, Path Dependence, and the Study of Politics." *American Political Science Review* 94(2): 251–67.

    2004. *Politics in Time: History, Institutions, and Social Analysis*. Princeton: Princeton University Press.

    2016. "Power in Historical Institutionalism." In Orfeo Fioretos, Tulia Falleti and Alan Sheingate, eds., *Handbook of Historical Institutionalism*, Oxford: Oxford University Press.

Piore, Michael J. and Andrew Schrank. 2008. "Toward Managed Flexibility: The Revival of Labour Inspection in the Latin World." *International Labour Review* 147(1): 1–23.

Post, Alison E. 2014. *Foreign and Domestic Investment in Argentina: The Politics of Privatized Infrastructure*. Cambridge: Cambridge University Press.

Post, Alison and M. Victoria Murillo. 2016. "How Investors' Portfolios Shape Regulatory Outcomes." *World Development* 77: 328–345.

Remmer, Karen L. 2008. "The Politics in Institutional Change: Electoral Reform in Latin America, 1978–2002." *Party Politics* 14(1): 5–30.

Roberts, Kenneth M. 2014. *Changing Course in Latin America*. Cambridge: Cambridge University Press.

Roberts, Kenneth M. and Erik Wibbels. 1999. "Party Systems and Electoral Volatility in Latin America: A Test of Economic, Institutional, and Structural Explanations." *American Political Science Review*, Vol. 93 (3), 575–590.

Rodríguez Garavito, César. 2011. "Ethnicity.gov: Global Governance, Indigenous Peoples, and the Right to Prior Consultation in Social Minefields." *Indiana Journal of Global Legal Studies* 18(1): 263–305.

Rodrik, Dani. 2000. "Institutions for High-quality Growth: What They Are and How to Acquire Them." *Studies in Comparative International Development* 35(3): 3–31.

Rogowski, Ronald. 1987. "Trade and the Variety of Democratic Institutions." *International Organization* 41(2): 203–23.

Rokkan, Stein. 1970. *Citizens, Elections, Parties: Approaches to the Comparative Study of the Process of Development*. Oslo: Universitetsforlaget.

Ronconi, Lucas. 2010. "Enforcement and Compliance with Labor Regulations in Argentina." *ILR Review* 64(4): 719–36.

Ross, Michael. 1999. "The Political Economy of the Resource Curse." *World Politics* 51/2: 297–322.

Sabet, Daniel M. 2014. "Co-Production and Oversight: Citizens and Their Police." *Working Paper Series on Civic Engagement and Public Security in Mexico.* Available at www.wilsoncenter.org/sites/default/files/sabet_co-production _oversight_0.pdf.

Sachs, Jeffrey and Andrew Warner. 2001. "The Curse of Natural Resources." *European Economic Review* 45: 827–838.

Saffon, Maria Paula and Juan Gonzalez Bertomeu. Forthcoming. "What/whose Property Rights? The Selective Enforcement of Land Rights under Mexican Liberalism in Mexico." In Daniel M. Brinks, Steven Levitsky and M. Victoria Murillo, eds., *Understanding Institutional Weakness: Lessons from Latin America.* New York: Cambridge University Press.

Schedler, Andreas, Larry Jay Diamond, and Marc F. Plattner. 1999. *The Self-Restraining State: Power and Accountability in New Democracies.* Boulder: Lynne Rienner Publishers.

Schickler, Eric. 2001. *Disjointed Pluralism: Institutional Innovation and the Development of the U.S. Congress.* Princeton: Princeton University Press.

Schrank, Andrew. 2009. "Professionalization and Probity in a Patrimonial State: Labor Inspectors in the Dominican Republic." *Latin American Politics and Society* 51(2): 91–115.

2011. "Co-producing Workplace Transformation: The Dominican Republic in Comparative Perspective." *Socio-Economic Review* 9(2): 419–45.

Forthcoming. "Imported Institutions: Boon or Bane in the Developing World?" In Daniel M. Brinks, Steven Levitsky and M. Victoria Murillo, eds., *Understanding Institutional Weakness: Lessons from Latin America.* New York: Cambridge University Press.

Shepsle, Kenneth A. 1989. "Studying Institutions: Some Lessons from the Rational Choice Approach." *Journal of Theoretical Politics* 1(2): 131–47.

Sieder, Rachel, Line Schjolden and Alan Angell. 2005. *The Judicialization of Politics in Latin America.* New York: Palgrave Macillan.

Soifer, Hillel David. 2015. *State Building in Latin America.* Cambridge: Cambridge University Press.

Spiller, Pablo T. and Mariano Tommasi. 2007. *The Institutional Foundations of Public Policy in Argentina.* Cambridge: Cambridge University Press.

Streeck, Wolfgang and Kathleen Thelen. 2005. "Introduction: Institutional Change in Advanced Political Economies." In Wolfgang Streeck and Kathleen Thelen, eds., *Beyond Continuity.* New York: Oxford University Press.

Surnarayan, Pavithra. 2016. *Hollowing Out the State: Status Inequality, Fiscal Capacity, and Right-Wing Voting in India.* PhD Dissertation. Columbia University.

Surnarayan, Pavithra and Steven White. 2018. "Slavery, Reconstruction, and Bureaucratic Capacity in the American South," unpublished manuscript.

Thelen, Kathleen. 2004. *How Institutions Evolve: The Political Economy of Skills in Germany, Britain, the United States, and Japan.* Cambridge: Cambridge University Press.

Thompson, José. 2016. "El Derecho a la Consulta Previa, Libre e Informada: Una mirada crítica desde los pueblos indígenas." Edited by Instituto Interamericano de Derechos Humanos. San José: Instituto Interamericano de Derechos Humanos.

Torres Wong, Marcela. 2018. "Prior Consultation and the Defense of Indigenous Lands in Latin America." In R. Zurayk, E. Woertz, and R. Bahn eds., *Crisis and Conflict in Agriculture.* Oxford: CABI.

Truber, David M. and Marc Galanter. 1974. "Scholars in Self-Estrangement: Some Reflections on the Crisis in Law and Development Studies in the United States." *Wisconsin Law Review* 1974(4): 1062–103.

Van de Walle, Nicholas. 2001. *African Economies and the Politics of Permanent Crisis, 1979–1999.* Cambridge: Cambridge University Press.

Weaver, Julie Anne. 2017. "Voting, Citizen Engagement and Political Accountability in Municipal Politics: The Case of Peru." Paper presented at the Annual Meeting of the Latin American Studies Association (LASA) International Congress, Lima, Peru, April 2017.

Weyland, Kurt. 2002. *The Politics of Market Reform in Fragile Democracies: Argentina, Brazil, Peru, and Venezuela.* Princeton: Princeton University Press.

Weyland, Kurt. 2009. "Institutional Change in Latin America: External Models and their Unintended Consequences." *Journal of Politics in Latin America* 1: 37–66.

Wilkie, James W. 1967. *The Mexican Revolution: Federal Expenditure and Social Change Since 1910.* Berkeley: University of California Press.

WOLA (Washington Office on Latin America). 2011. "Tackling Urban Violence in Latin America: Reversing Exclusion through Smart Policing and Social Investment," available at www.wola.org/analysis/tackling-urban-violence-in-latin-america-reversing-exclusion-through-smart-policing-and-social-investment/ published June 2011; (last visited on September 18, 2018).

Yashar, Deborah. 2018. *Homicidal Ecologies. Illicit Economies and Complicit States in Latin America.* Cambridge: Cambridge University Press.

Cambridge Elements ≡

Politics and Society in Latin America

Maria Victoria Murillo

Columbia University

Maria Victoria Murillo is Professor of Political Science and International Affairs at Columbia University. She is the author of *Political Competition, Partisanship, and Policymaking in the Reform of Latin American Public Utilities* (Cambridge, 2009). She is also editor of *Carreras Magisteriales, Desempeño Educativo y Sindicatos de Maestros en América Latina* (2003), and co-editor of *Argentine Democracy: the Politics of Institutional Weakness* (2005). She has published in edited volumes as well as in the *American Journal of Political Science, World Politics,* and *Comparative Political Studies,* among others.

Juan Pablo Luna

The Pontifical Catholic University of Chile

Juan Pablo Luna is Professor in the Department of Political Science at The Pontifical Catholic University of Chile. He is the author of *Segmented Representation. Political Party Strategies in Unequal Democracies,* and has co-authored *Latin American Party Systems* (Cambridge, 2010). His work on political representation, state capacity, and organized crime has appeared in *Comparative Political Studies, Revista de Ciencia Política, Journal of Latin American Studies, Latin American Politics and Society,* and *Studies in Comparative International Development,* among others.

Tulia G. Falleti

University of Pennsylvania

Tulia G. Falleti is the Class of 1965 Term Associate Professor of Political Science, Director of the Latin American and Latino Studies Program, and Senior Fellow of the Leonard Davis Institute for Health Economics at the University of Pennsylvania. She is the author of the award-winning *Decentralization and Subnational Politics in Latin America* (Cambridge, 2010). She is co-editor of *The Oxford Handbook of Historical Institutionalism,* among other edited books. Her articles have appeared in many edited volumes and journals such as *American Political Science Review* and *Comparative Political Studies.*

Andrew Schrank

Brown University

Andrew Schrank is the Olive C. Watson Professor of Sociology and International & Public Affairs at Brown University. His articles on business, labor, and the state in Latin America have appeared in *American Journal of Sociology, Comparative Politics, Comparative Political Studies, Latin American Politics & Society, Social Forces,* and *World Development,* among other journals, and co-authored *Root-Cause Regulation: Labor Inspection in Europe and the Americas* (2018).

About the Series

Latin American politics and society are at a crossroads, simultaneously confronting serious challenges and remarkable opportunities that are likely to be shaped by formal institutions and informal practices alike. The new Politics and Society in Latin America Cambridge Elements series will offer multidisciplinary and methodologically pluralist contributions on the most important topics and problems confronted by the region.

Cambridge Elements ☰

Politics and Society in Latin America

Elements in the Series

Understanding Institutional Weakness: Power and Design in Latin American Institutions
Daniel M. Brinks, Steven Levitsky, and Maria Victoria Murillo

A full series listing is available at: www.cambridge.org/PSLT

Printed in the United States
By Bookmasters